THE QUESTION

K. RICHTER

Paperback ISBN: 979-8-9999467-0-6

eBook ISBN: 979-8-9999467-1-3

Cover art by Susanne Panei

"And yet all these questions were not new questions suddenly confronting him, they were old familiar aches. It was long since they had first begun to grip and rend his heart. Long, long ago his anguish had its first beginnings; it had waxed and gathered strength, it had matured and concentrated, until it had taken the form of a fearful, frenzied, and fantastic question, which tortured his heart and mind, clamouring insistently for an answer."

-Dostoyevsky, *Crime and Punishment*

CONTENTS

PART I: ASKING THE QUESTION

INTRODUCTION

The Question is suicide. Yes or no? To not be, or to be? That is the Question.

Camus famously declared it to be the only really serious philosophical question. It is a question which is certain to arise in every person's life, and it is a question which every person will have to address in order to become mature. Who can have integrity in their own life, if they cannot state with certainty that they do not want to commit suicide?

The Question presents a challenge with many subtleties and peculiarities. Every person's Answer to the Question must be found individually; it cannot simply be read in a book or told to someone by someone else. Everyone is different, and as such, everyone will have different needs concerning the answering of the Question. One person's reasoning will not be sufficient for another person; every person will have an entirely different mental framework within which to address it. There are many pitfalls that a person may encounter when trying to address the Question: Some will insist on avoiding the Question, imagining that even thinking about the topic is unhealthy. Some will simply accept, as an axiom, that the answer to the question of suicide is no, as if this is a single, comprehensive answer that applies to all humanity, about which no further thought or argumentation is necessary. Some will distract themselves by swallowing someone else's ideological commandments, or by obsessing over phantasmagorial problems derived from their individual prejudices. And so on. Many people will find themselves forming an entire lifestyle based around their strategic avoidance of the Question, but this is not the way to any sort of satisfying life. To avoid the Question is counterproductive in itself: if a person has always avoided the issue, if a person has never truly thought about the question of suicide, how confident can they really be that their personal answer is no?

The Question must indeed be contemplated very thoroughly and very carefully by every person, neither overestimating nor underestimating any argument or inclination in either direction. Yes, even the inclinations towards suicide must not be brushed off, as much as one might like to imagine that such thoughts are simply "bad" or "unhealthy." They must be confronted directly and explicitly. One must be careful not to jump to conclusions, nor try to cut one's internal dialogue short. One should never assume that suicide is the kind of question that can be dismissed so easily. Such tactics of "cheating" when answering the Question will be fruitless, and an answer hastily constructed will quickly crumble when subjected to any amount of doubt; and the suicidal person's mind is full of doubt.

One could argue that the Question is the primary question of every person's life, because until it is answered, suicide will continue to linger as an option in the back of the mind, and with it, the threat of the person's premature destruction, the greatest possible threat; the thought that one's life is utterly worthless or even outright harmful will stubbornly persist if it is not soundly proven wrong. In such a proof, the answering of the Question is the establishment of an identity, a confirmation of one's direction in life. This is even the case for the sincerest and most justified suicidal person in the world – even for this person, whose circumstances would lead any reasonable person to recommend them straight to the grave, the ultimate decision is not one that should be made lightly, but weighed extremely carefully: for it is an act that cannot be taken back once performed, and a gamble where everything is at stake.

UNAVOIDABLE

For most people, it is impossible to live for more than a little while without encountering the Question. It is not uniformly caused by a particular issue, such as destitution or subjugation at the hands of some abuser. It does not occur exclusively in the physically or mentally ill. Living in a more "developed" nation will not immunize a person from the tendency to experience it. It is a universal phenomenon, a fundamental part of the human experience, to confront the Question.

The Question can arise in a person's mind in any circumstance of sufficient stress; for any given person, there are plenty of contingent circumstances which are so stressful, so extraordinarily painful compared to the normal conditions of their life, that they bring the question of suicide to the point of consciousness. Such a circumstance might occur at any moment, sometimes precipitated by causes knowable in advance, sometimes through random accident. But this moment is only the introduction of the Question to the forefront of one's thoughts – in reality, suicide is such a fundamental concept that every person who has ever taken the time to contemplate themselves as a human being will have the thought of it, to some degree, present in the mind. This is absolutely natural for such a fundamental question – it is the question of whether one's own existence is tolerable or not, it is the question of whether one's life has meaning, and it is many other questions about an individual: the Question itself is the aggregate of every question that a person has about their life and their role in the world, and asks, in summary, should this life be discarded or not? Again, it must be emphasized that this is an absolutely fundamental question, a natural one for a healthy person to ask themselves. The confrontation of the Question is the "bottom line," so to speak, of any person's evaluation of their own life. Any person with any integrity as a human being will have the ability to consciously answer it, if the thought should occur to them; because every such person has certainly confronted it and contemplated it in great detail already, in the course of their coming-to-terms with their own lives and their own mortality. How could a person be well-adjusted, living in grace with the world, if it is unknown to them whether the overall value of their life lies above or below the threshold for destruction?

This appraisal of the Question as a fundamental aspect of the human experience runs contrary to the fearful attitude which the topic of suicide would invoke in polite conversation. While it's reasonable to shy away from suicide as a subject of small talk, a person should not carry over this attitude of shying-away into their own individual contemplations. A person, observing that their train of thought has drifted to the topic of suicide, should not immediately recoil in horror and attempt to distract themselves. This is especially important in the cases where a person has never before seriously considered the Question – once again, how can a person have integrity in their own life if they cannot even state with certainty that they do not want to commit suicide? A person who has never really thought about it *cannot* state such a thing with certainty. A person should have an Answer to the Question – and therefore, a person should not be afraid to contemplate The Question, to analyze it, to investigate every facet of it, in order to determine exactly what their personal Answer is.

In response to a person pondering suicide, it would be easy to say, as some kind of universal axiom, "the answer to the Question is no in all cases, obviously you shouldn't kill yourself." A person could list dozens, even hundreds of perfectly good reasons why committing suicide is a bad idea, and conclude that there is never a good reason to commit suicide in the face of those reasons. There's only one problem: the suicidal person does not care about any of those reasons. Reasons to live which are solely an articulation of the intellect will not appeal to the emotions of the person who is truly struggling between life and death, this battle taking place in darker and more primitive depths of the soul than reason can reach on its own. Something more comprehensive than a mere logical argument is required to bring a person back from the edge.

SUPPORT

The issue of dealing with suicidal persons is well-known as a touchy and inconvenient subject. This is because, while it is possible to help a person deal with certain particular problems related to their mental state, the root of the issue - the answering of the Question - is something that no one can directly help. It is a question that is too deep to be answered by another person, too deep and too personal. It is the judgment of an entire life, and it cannot be adequately judged except by the person who has lived that life, and who presently carries the responsibility for it. Even if some suicidal person had some especially close friend or family member as their confidant, that friend still could not answer the Question on behalf of that person - partially because the person in question almost certainly has some secrets, some inner demons, that he refuses to tell even this close friend about, but mostly because the friend is another person, someone "on the outside," someone with their own method of reasoning, someone with their own distinct set of personal conceptualizations and values. The words of another can never be accepted with the surety of the words one searches for, reasons through, and concludes for oneself. The individual must confront the Question individually, and come to a conclusion through their own reasoning, through deep contemplation, in complete solitude - no one else's reasoning will serve as more than a short-lasting analgesic.

There are times when short-lasting analgesics are useful, of course. If the person in question seems to be unprepared to confront the Question, it may be reasonable in some situations to simply tell them, plain and simple, "you should not commit suicide," as a parent consoles a child. But to insist upon this one statement and leave it at that, as an axiom, as the end of the story, allowing no further argument, allowing no further thought, as a parent *commands* a child, is a grave mistake. Such an approach fails to account for every idea, every thought, every temptation, every element that makes suicide more appealing, which this commanding person would have the suicidal person utterly ignore. These ideas, if left unacknowledged, if simply pushed to the side on the grounds that it is "unhealthy" or "bad" to even think about them, will not simply disappear; even if a person is comforted through therapeutic means, relieved of their negative emotions, and led into a more comfortable state of life in general, these thoughts will not simply go away. Rather, in some moment of intense stress, when that level of comfort eventually fades away, these thoughts will return, stronger than ever, more tempting than ever, and will be all the more likely to lead the upset person into dangerous realms of thought. This is doubly the case for the kind of thoughts which stem from some unacknowledged issue, which remains unacknowledged during this little relaxation period – for unacknowledged issues unavoidably tend to get worse. If an ignored issue tempts a person towards suicide once, how much more powerfully will it tempt them later, when the issue has gotten even worse due to their continued failure to confront it? Not to mention, because this person *knows* they failed to confront the issue, their negative emotion will be compounded by their guilt. There is a tangible danger to the deliberate putting-off of the Question; the "strategy" of putting off the Question exacerbates the very danger it is meant to prevent.

Another important principle to bear in mind when trying to offer help is that a person may not want to be helped at all. It is tempting to imagine that the suicidal person should be helped even if they do not seem to want it, "for their own good" as it were, but this too is a mistake – at least, it can be. If a person is engaged in an intense inner conflict, an argument of life and death, then an external force which attempts to settle the argument artificially may lead to the "unresolved ideas" scenario described above, or worse, the would-be benefactor could be perceived as hostile. The latter case is especially dangerous, because it's not out of the question that a person may mentally conflate the external party and their argument: namely, if a person arguing against suicide is seen as "interfering" or "troublesome," life itself may be considered all the more as something "interfering" or "troublesome." Bear in mind, though, that this primarily applies to people whose idea of "helping" means "trying to get the person to stop thinking about their problems." Care must be taken to choose the right time, place, and method of help; and no one would deny that, in many circumstances, helping a person to confront specific issues in life (as opposed to the contemplation of suicide at large) can be beneficial. But when it comes to the direct confrontation of the deepest, hardest questions, all a true friend can offer is careful, measured advice, an open ear, and the means to a constructive, critical, honest discussion. This is the kind of help necessary to aid the suffering person through their difficult psychological ordeal.

IMPETUS

The impetus of the suicidal urge in a person's life can occur in a number of ways. Ignoring the special cases of euthanasia and martyrdom (both of which will be discussed shortly), there are two major categories. This is a naïve set of descriptions, not at all rigorous, but it should hopefully prove useful to convey the basic ideas.

The first category is a "breach of equilibrium" – a sudden change in a person's life, radically for the worse (or at least perceived as being radically for the worse). If a person was once living a comfortable life, or at least a tolerable life, and all of a sudden, the manner of living they were used to is no longer available, then the thing that they considered "their life" essentially no longer exists, and has been replaced with a strange new life, something painful and unfamiliar. It is no wonder that in such situations, the Question will often occur to a person. It is totally natural in such a situation for a person to want to reevaluate the notion of whether their life is worth living. If they do not have an overarching principle by which they can live their life, some aspiration or direction which they can pursue even under radically different life circumstances, consideration of suicide becomes even more likely.

One practically universal example of a breach of equilibrium would be the transition from childhood to adulthood. The comfort of childhood is ended; an avalanche of responsibility takes its place. New responsibilities bring new anxieties, which the child cannot defer to the parents (at least, not for long). The child's perspective of being "taken care of" disappears; the adult must now "take care of" everything themselves. Life has abruptly transformed into something far more difficult. The fact that teenagers and young adults often find themselves contemplating the Question is not at all surprising.

The second category is an "intolerable equilibrium" – a situation in which a person realizes that they have settled into, and have long been maintaining, a life equilibrium which is either outright painful or a tedious exercise in futility. This could come about in a couple of ways. A person might have experienced some kind of sharp decline, as in the "breach of equilibrium" scenario, and studiously ignored the relevant issues, ignoring them so insistently that the presence of this issue simply became a part of their new equilibrium. Alternately, a person might have reached this low state of existence through a more gradual process of decline, many smaller breaches into progressively worse states of equilibrium.

Equilibrium is a fundamental concept, and there will be further discussion of it later in this book. In a literal sense, every living thing must maintain a sort of equilibrium, or homeostasis, within its own body. In parallel, the urge to maintain a sort of equilibrium in one's life, in one's behaviors, is a very powerful and fundamental psychological force. It is so powerful that phenomena like Stockholm Syndrome emerge – sometimes, when a person is captured and tormented, the victim eventually begins to sympathize with the captor, and grows dependent on the routine activities of their unfortunate circumstances. The urge to escape or seek relief declines or even disappears – the tendency toward equilibrium can overpower the pursuit of pleasure. The mental framing of a situation as "the new equilibrium" or "the new normal" has a tendency to transform what a person expects into what a person wants, even when what a person expects is unpleasant. This phenomenon can also occur when one has placed *oneself* into an unfavorable, "confined" set of circumstances, literally or metaphorically. This is how bad habits are formed, for instance. Repeat an activity often enough and it becomes habit, even if it is not actually enjoyable. When this process occurs unconsciously (as it often does – what kind of idiot would consciously try to make their life more boring, or more painful?), the conscious individual will find themselves asking "why do I keep doing this to myself?" And in spite of this conscious awareness of the problem, bad habits can be very difficult to break. This example is meant to illustrate the remarkable psychological power of the tendency towards equilibrium – a tendency, something even more fundamental than a desire or urge. In *Beyond the Pleasure Principle,* Freud speculated that this primordial tendency toward equilibrium in living things could be modeled as an instinct that specifically seeks out *death itself,* a return to inanimate matter, a return to equilibrium on a molecular level.

DESIRE TO DIE

The desire to commit suicide itself can occur in various ways, as an intellectual phenomenon or a more tangible, corporeal sensation. Intellectual manifestations would consist of thoughts, ideas, things intellectually conceived and reasoned through logically, propositions suggesting that the individual is worthless, harmful to others, self-destructive, parasitic, or otherwise having either poor character or poor ability to function. This may involve contemplation of past actions that seem unforgivable, and the notion that the individual has ruined their life, either by direct harm to the body, harm to the reputation, or something else that is difficult or impossible to repair. In a more extreme case, a person might develop the idea that human life as a whole is undesirable, e.g., from an extreme environmentalist perspective. These kinds of desires involve the use of some sort of "reasoning" process to conclude (in the sense that one concludes a syllogism) that one's life should be brought to an end. In contrast to the intellectual type is the corporeal type: it's possible to experience the desire for death on a more immediate level, which does not involve any kind of mental justification, but instead a direct reaction to sensory experience. The most obvious example of this would be chronic pain, or some other sort of uncomfortable sensation which, unrelieved, becomes maddening. If not physical pain, psychological phenomena such as constant panic attacks, delusions, or hallucinations could all be sensations that one could become desperate to escape, if no means of curing them are evidently available. There is even simple weariness with life, the sensation of exhaustion with the unending responsibilities of life, as if they require more energy than one can possibly muster, and which makes the thought of simply doing away with it all, resigning from life, seems like the logical option. Again, these are not intellectual mental processes; they come from the fundamental wish for relief from pain or stress. That said, the intellect may reinforce these feelings by rationalizing the desire for death that they bring to mind.

The more intellectual manifestations of the desire to die involve, at some point, a kind of self-hatred, a negative attitude toward the self which is justified and conceived "rationally," as one might narrate and explain to oneself through an internal monologue. Because of the inherent possibility of contradiction in ideas of "self-hatred" or, more broadly, "self-denial," it's important to remember to think, when you find yourself in the midst of this "reasoning," what exactly you are talking about. Someone not thinking too carefully about why they hate themselves could trap themselves in a state of tunnel vision, focusing on the almost self-indulgent desire to cling to the sensation of hatred and misery, and not acknowledging the full scope of their own feelings and/or situation; denying reality is not the right path forward in any case, even in those cases where suicide might be justifiable.

Probably the most common type of self-hatred is a reactive type, the conscience reacting negatively, with guilt or shame, self-hatred as a reaction to one's past actions, which one sees as unacceptable, unforgivable, or intolerable (i.e., to bear in one's memory). It could be that a person experiencing this emotion is "correct," so to speak – perhaps they have indeed committed some kind of monstrous act, and are feeling an appropriate emotional response as a consequence. On the other hand, a person might just be highly emotionally sensitive, and feel something like self-hatred every time they do something that they find "incompatible" with the way they would like to perceive themselves. It's also possible that a person might be obsessed with some kind of image, ideology, or aesthetic, to the degree of worshipping it, and this person might hate themselves whenever their natural inclinations deviate from this image, this ideal, that they have imagined that they "have to" follow. Parts III and IV will go into the psychology of this in further detail.

I've also heard of what must be a much more uncommon kind of self-hatred: a bizarre pattern of thought in which the object of hatred is not one's own past behaviors, but *oneself* on the ultimate level. Each person imagines themselves in a certain way, and every person with a conscience has some concept of their "true self," their ideal self, which is virtuous and good – that is, that they have goodness inside of them. It is from the perspective of this conceptual self, this "true self," that the person judges their own behaviors, and it is the observation of inadequacy in one's actual behaviors *compared to the conceptual self* that produces the negative emotion involved in the reactive type of self-hatred. But this conceptual self-hatred is totally different: the person hates themselves *conceptually,* they hate themselves *in concept*. If reactive self-hatred says, "I am behaving badly," with the implication of "but this isn't the real me; I can improve," then conceptual self-hatred says, "I am fundamentally a bad person, and I can never improve." There is something oxymoronic, something self-contradicting, in this sentiment. If the conceptual self is always wrong, then can the conceptual statement "I am always wrong" even be trusted?

The sensory-type manifestations of the desire to die are more straightforward. One that will be familiar to many people is weariness, the sensation of being overwhelmed and exhausted by life, the stress of the tasks necessary simply to maintain one's life. People with grueling, monotonous jobs are an obvious example of people susceptible to this, as well as people in difficult relationship situations – for instance, being dependent on an abusive person, or having a dependent who is very difficult to care for. Sufferers of psychological disorders or physical disorders that cause chronic stress, anxiety, disturbed thoughts, outright pain, or other forms of discomfort also fall into this category.

Note that almost all of these phenomena, both the sensory and intellectual, can be caused, at least hypothetically, by living an unhealthy lifestyle – especially the more tangible, visceral, bodily ones. Having a poor diet, some vitamin deficiency, a poor sleep schedule, being excessively dependent on drugs (illicit or otherwise), getting little or no exercise; all of these things could easily, at the very least, exacerbate any of the symptoms listed in the above paragraphs, not to speak of causing them directly – by being inattentive to these things as causes of suffering, a person could easily become driven by entirely avoidable causes to such a point of suffering that suicide becomes a tempting option. If a person is truly living a horrible, miserable life, then experiencing negative emotions and thoughts along the lines of "I'm living a horrible, miserable life" is perfectly warranted; it's the correct emotional response. Then again, there are also occasions where a person might feel these things for an unwarranted reason: some kind of mental disorder could cause these symptoms, or they might appear as the side effect of a drug, or possibly even for dietary reasons. Most of the manifestations described could be, in other words, warranted or unwarranted, natural or anomalous. There is one exception: conceptual self-hatred is never warranted. It's always unwarranted because it's inherently self-contradictory: it consists of the theory that a person's *character* is totally unrecoverable, totally beyond hope for improvement. This is different from a person's body, lifestyle, or reputation being unsalvageable; to say that your own character, your own personality, your own self-in-concept is irredeemable is to essentially say "I am always wrong" – a paradox. And a person who is capable of judging their own actions as good or bad, and who acknowledges that they have made bad choices when good ones were possible, is shown, by their very accusations towards themselves, to be *capable of discerning good from bad, and capable of making good choices.* A second paradox. Once this kind of self-contradicting statement appears, it's time to step back and start over, because it's obvious that something has gone awry in the "reasoning" process. Either the person has fallen for some kind of ideological propaganda or abusive rhetoric (along the lines of "you must have such-and-such character traits in order to be a good person, and if you don't, you are so horrible that you deserve to die") or, if the conceptual self-hatred appears in the form of intrusive thoughts, the person is suffering from either a mental disorder or perhaps a side effect of some kind of brain-affecting drug. Or, of course, it might not be a belief held sincerely in the first place – but only a kind of self-defeating anti-life mantra, used to justify a more visceral, emotional desire to die.

REASONS TO LIVE

In contrast to the list of reasons why a person might want to die, is it possible to create a list of reasons not to die? Yes, certainly; entire books have been written for this purpose. But in spite of the fact that such reasons can be "rationally" constructed, and explained to a person in a "rational" sense (even one that the person in question would agree is a soundly constructed argument), it is far from certain that the suicidal person will actually care about these reasons, or be truly convinced of them. For many of them, a general principle of "suicide is bad," no matter how thoroughly argued for, will not be enough; what they require is a reason why *they themselves* should not end it all, and a true, personal Answer is not something that a well-wishing friend will be able to provide at a moment's notice, as an instant cure-all.

This is not helped by the fact that a lot of common "reasons" against suicide that a person might state (to others or to themselves) are completely bogus, not actually robust enough to stand up to scrutiny. Some people try to develop a quick and easy answer to the Question along these lines, and from that moment on try to think no more about it. This creates the dangerous situation where a person does not have any actual reasons to live, but only excuses: what happens when those excuses run out? Suppose, for example, a person simply is not inclined toward suicide because life seems comfortable to them, and they half-heartedly justify their life by saying something like "I don't want to commit suicide because life is good." What happens when that comfort runs out? No human being is exempt from suffering. The reason for living disappears. What happens when a person dedicates their entire life to a cause, being unwaveringly faithful and wholly invested in it, only to find that that cause was only a con, the work of an unscrupulous scam artist? The reason for living disappears. And so on.

To develop an Answer to the Question is to develop a reason to live. It is the objective of this book to investigate and critically analyze the various types of answers that people develop to address the Question, as well as making a basic exploration of the relevant psychological and cultural phenomena. When it comes to answering the Question, nothing but the very best will do. Every "answer" that cannot stand up to skepticism, every "reason for living" that hinges on unstable assumptions, must be discarded. Everything superficial, everything insubstantial, every excuse, every lie, every concession, everything unsatisfactory: remove these things, and what remains? What is it that can stand up to the harshest critique? What is it that remains solid when everything else crumbles? What are the answers to the big questions, which so many people are afraid to even ask, let alone answer? Who can say with absolute confidence that they know what they are living for – and, for that matter, what are such people living for? Who are the ones who have risen above mediocrity and excuse-making, and the mere maintenance of some equilibrium, some inadequate status quo? Who are the ones who know what they want, who do what they want, and who achieve what they want?

RISK

Throughout the course of this book, it may appear from time to time that the goal is to discourage suicide entirely. In Part II, for example, it will be explained in further detail that refusing to properly address the Question exacerbates the very issue that it is meant to solve. What is this issue, what is this problem that ought to be avoided? The suicidal urge, or even suicide itself? Certainly not. The risk which is increased by such things is the risk of a *hasty* suicide, a suicide made in a moment of passion, a suicide not adequately contemplated, a life destroyed for an ultimately stupid reason. To say that suicide should be rejected *per se* would be to stop the train of thought, to refuse to admit critical thinking into the situation, to insist unilaterally that the Question has already been answered once and for all. Here is a concrete counterexample: it is a fact that there exist certain situations where any reasonable person could consider suicide to be the correct option, or at least an understandable one, that is, *not* an utterly unacceptable one; generally, these situations fall into the categories of martyrdom or euthanasia.

Martyrdom is suicide in service of some higher ideal. This includes such cases as the prisoner of war who chooses death over defecting, the defendant who chooses to be executed by a corrupt court in order to show its corruption to the public (as opposed to humoring it with a defense, or trying to escape), and revolutionaries who deliberately kill themselves (either slowly, as by hunger strike, or quickly, as by suicide bombing) for the achievement of political ends. The situations that would drive a person to become a martyr voluntarily are complex, and a reasonable person may or may not agree that death is the preferable option in each case; but in every case, there is an *object* to the act of suicide, there is a *point* to it, something to be achieved by it, it is not merely an act of surrender from the difficulties of the world. In this sense, voluntary martyrdom is clearly differentiated from what you might call ordinary suicide.

Euthanasia is the decision to end a life that is chronically ill or disabled to the point of being plausibly beyond all hope of recovery, having no real ability to achieve anything, and with the continuation of life being a burden on the individual in question and their caretakers should it be allowed to continue. This is the kind of situation where suicide as a resignation from life is considered warranted, not just from the individual's perspective, but from the perspective of the people around them, including their healthcare providers. There does come a point where a person is justified in saying "there's nothing that can be done." At this point, a number of stereotypical arguments against suicide, which concern a person's potential to achieve things, cease to apply entirely.

In these two special situations, there's a case to be made that a person's suicide is warranted. But to commit an unwarranted suicide, the suicide of a person who still has potential to achieve what they want in life, and who achieves nothing by dying, is a massive waste. The suicidal person must first test and exhaust every single possibility, even the most radical possibilities, for improving their life, or for taking their life in a different direction in which improvement may come about – because the alternative is suicide itself, the most radical and irreversible possibility, the finalization of failure.

Importantly, though, a suicidal person whose situation is outside the realm of either martyrdom or euthanasia should *not* immediately jump to the conclusion that their own suicide is unjustifiable solely on this account. A convincing argument to that effect might be made from a logical standpoint, but the real issue is that, as explained before, the suicidal person does not care about merely logical arguments against suicide; suicidal ideation occurs on a deeper level of the mind than the rational, and it cannot be dealt with using logic alone. Even if an argument of this sort can be accepted tentatively, it will not protect a person from the suicidal urge if it should come back with a vengeance in the future, when life has become even less tolerable. A comprehensive journey of self-discovery must be taken in order to construct a truly convincing case, the individual analyzing the self at every level and from every perspective – because the Question is the ultimate judgment of the self, aggregated from all levels and all perspectives.

There is one more risk to take note of: It is possible to choose not to commit suicide, and then to live a completely wasted life. It is possible to commit suicide by old age. If no substantial activity occurs between the decision to live and the point of death, even if the death occurs of natural causes many decades later, the outcome in the long term is equivalent to suicide. A hasty decision to live is only slightly less wasteful than a hasty decision to die. It is slightly less wasteful because the person who chooses to live will have more time to experience life, to change as a person, and to perhaps stumble upon a reason to live of their own accord. But the odds of stumbling upon such a thing are very low; for almost everyone, they must be sought out, and this is a process requiring actual work, not just waiting. A person can survive for a long time without living, perhaps for their whole life. If the deliberate effort that living entails is put off today, is there any reason to believe that it will be easier tomorrow, when the habit of not living has had an entire extra day to ingrain itself further into the mind? The life that you want will not be bestowed on you automatically. Do what is necessary, then, to not merely survive, but live.

PART II: FAILING TO ANSWER

DISMISSING

Because of the gravity of the Question, many people to try to avoid it outright. To acknowledge it is to admit that something is not right with one's life, and that either a breach in equilibrium (associated with fear of change), sustainment of the present equilibrium (associated with fear of stagnation), or death (associated with fear of death, of course) are the only options. Not to mention the bizarre fear that some people have of admitting that they have done something wrong in the first place. It's not a small number of people that end up trying to distract themselves from the Question altogether in order to avoid this dilemma, but unfortunately for all of them, the decision to put off the decision *is itself a decision*, a decision to stagnate, perhaps even to degrade. Could a person making this decision defend it, if the nature of their choice was brought to their attention? To choose ignorance, when everything is at stake, is indefensible. The only conceivable positive outcome one could hope for, in ignoring the Question, is that perhaps whatever problem is causing the person to lose confidence in life might go away on its own. But there's no reason to believe anything like that will ever happen. In life, how many problems ignored actually do go away? The decision to avoid the Question altogether is a gamble, a gamble on one's ability to perpetually fool oneself, to keep oneself eternally distracted from the most important and fundamental question of one's very existence, to let the entire concept of one's purpose remain undefined indefinitely, and to merely hope that perhaps one's life will end up becoming good at some point by chance. And in this situation, yes, it would have to be by chance, it would have to be an accident from some external cause, because it certainly can't be the willfully ignorant individual who effects the change – how could a person live a good life if they don't know what a good life would be to them? If a person can't even say with certainty whether their life is good enough to not be destroyed, how can they really say they know what they want out of life?

As patently foolish as it is to deliberately ignore the Question, let's not pretend that it doesn't happen – let's not underestimate the power of the human mind to rationalize. Any decision, however foolish, can be rationalized by a mind that is motivated enough, especially when motivated by something powerful and primordial, such as fear or greed. There are a few ways that the Question may be ignored, involving different levels of this sort of rationalization. The most blatant way would be total, deliberate ignorance: the sustainment of a continuous stream of distractions from both the Question and any thoughts about making a substantial change for the better (which, of course, would entail acknowledgement of the relevant problems). Sustaining a life of this sort involves constant rationalization of inaction, constant denial of one's own ability to tangibly improve, and perhaps even denial of one's very desire to do so. Another method is a sort of axiomatic approach, holding with absolute certainty in one's mind that the answer to the Question is always "no," that suicide is always wrong and no further consideration is required. This requires the typical rationalizations associated with maintaining any ideology-esque axiom, and refusing to admit any argument contrary to it. Finally, there is a more subtle technique: assuming the conclusion, assuming that the answer to the Question is "no," and working backwards from there to rationalize reasons why it's wrong. This isn't an unreasonable approach, and it can be used toward productive ends, but problems can arise if it is only used haphazardly, incompletely. Each of these behaviors will be discussed in detail individually, and each of their pitfalls spelled out. The types of characters who exemplify these behaviors will also be illustrated; the reader is encouraged to picture these characters in order to gain an understanding of what failure to answer the Question really means: not just what it sounds like, described in rational terms, but what it looks like.

COLD AND CAREFREE

To begin, what can we say about the perspective of the person who refuses to acknowledge the Question outright, who fails to make even the most rudimentary attempt at an answer? What can we infer about such a person's character? This is the person who, having not critically analyzed their own position in life and the viability of death as an option, is lacking in their use of critical thinking. It is simultaneously someone who is lacking in direction, having not determined, through a careful analysis of their options, what, if anything, is important enough to pursue in lieu of suicide. This is not a good combination. At this intersection is a person who does not have any kind of long-term plan, and who is not self-conscious enough to want to make one. The product of this is a sort of cold nature: not necessarily coldness in the sense of being socially distant or emotionally inexpressive, but coldness in the sense of having no passion, no taste, cold in the sense of having no *joie de vivre*, of being content to be thrown about by life's various happenings, of having no personality beyond trivial, hackneyed opinions about whatever piece of media has been most recently broadcast to them.

This quality of coldness is a very ugly personality trait. The cold person has no actual interests, no actual desires, only a large pile of momentary whims, fake desires, which are rapidly thrown onto the person by popular culture's never-ending avalanche of novelties (or those of some fringe culture, if they're inclined toward it), and these whims just as quickly pass away once their novelty is lost. They have no permanence, they are not "the person's interests" in any real, lasting sense. The person could therefore be said to have no interests. One might go even further and say that the person's identity does not exist, in the sense that their "identity" consists of nothing of their own, but only reflections of their rapidly-passing preoccupations (not even interests, and certainly not passions) concerning things sent to them from the outside world. If there is some real desire for achievement or action somewhere within them, some small flame of passion, that desire is neglected and buried under excuses and distractions, under statements like "I'm just a normal person, I can't do something great like that." How many millions of people, living in rich nations, having embarrassing amounts of knowledge and computational power and access to goods and many other resources at their fingertips, bury themselves alive in such statements! To escape these self-defeating mantras and actually do *something,* not even necessarily something amazing, just *something* of *some* kind of worth, would be enough to make an average citizen into something almost superhuman, almost a miracle worker, in comparison to the rabble that they consider themselves doomed to remain a part of.

To refuse one's passions and remain cold is to be self-denying. And not self-denying in some kind of spiritual sense of "resisting earthly temptations" – self-denying in the sense of insisting, through inaction, on one's own worthlessness and non-presence. Suicide could be described the final act of self-denial, the person not only insisting on their lack of worth, but making an irreparable decision to ensure that they will *never* gain any worth. In this sense, the person who remains cold becomes, while still alive, akin to a dead body, a body dead by suicide. Unpleasant though this may sound to the optimistic readers, it is entirely possible for a person to live a whole lifetime and *never* gain any value, and *never* contribute anything of worth to the world. In a cold person's more self-aware moments, they may say to themselves, "Well, I may not have any value now, but I might gain some in the future. Therefore, it's better not to commit suicide." But to make a statement like that and proceed to *not change anything,* to continue impersonating a dead body, is the path to committing suicide by old age. Insistence on an inactive lifestyle is, if not an attempt at suicide, at best a gamble on the vain hope that someday, something from some external source will cause one's mind to spontaneously be changed, a hope that some kind of grand ordeal or adventure will present itself and force the person to become mature and make a positive change, and develop value of some sort. But despite the fact that this will never happen, that such things occur only in fairy tales, many a person will gamble away each of their precious days, betting on this useless hope, and remaining cold for a whole lifetime, waiting, waiting, doing nothing whatsoever but waiting for death to arrive and relieve them of the hassle of life.

Note, however, an important counterpart to the cold character: this is the carefree character, who has never wrestled with the question of suicide simply because it has never occurred to them, because life is naturally pleasurable to them. Like the cold person, they also live their life according to their whims and first instincts; but, unlike the cold person, this person's first instincts lead them to productivity and enjoyment, rather than stagnation and impotence. Due to their happenstance of having "better" instincts, the carefree person has much more of a passion for life, and will get much more out of it than the cold person – while the good times last. This person is even able to avoid the unpleasant personality traits criticized in the next few sections – while the good times last. The carefree person has a sort of Sword of Damocles hanging over their head; if the pleasure and comfort that they rely on should be taken away, and there isn't any carefully-thought-through reason to live underneath, their entire reason to live, any "self-affirmation" and "passion" they have, will shatter. No one is immune to suffering. Though the carefree person isn't likely to feel the same insecurity and dread that the cold person does, the former nonetheless has a responsibility to deal with the same underlying flaw as the latter: thinking properly about the big questions of life and death, caring about them in a proper sense, and answering them. Better to do this ahead of time than to wait until after the Sword of Damocles falls. To be too carefree is to not care at all; matters of life and death are worth caring about.

HEDONISM

The ostensible first step up from no goals and no aspirations whatsoever is a general goal of pleasure. This is actually not an unreasonable goal. Probably not as the central purpose of life, of course, but just a general goal, one part of a person's set of goals in life. The ordinary pleasures of life are fine and should be appreciated; one should have a degree of trust in one's own emotions and senses, and pleasure deserves its share of respect. One could even make the case that the achievements of all goals are in service of pleasure, since the sensation of achievement is one of the highest and most satisfying forms of pleasure, thinking in the long term. If this is the case, then the pursuit of pleasure is one and the same as the pursuit of what is noble in life.

While it's easy to imagine a hedonist as some kind of non-thinking cold or carefree character, a person only motivated by their momentary whims, this is not the case. It is the way an individual uses their intelligence and abilities that determines how effectively the goal of pleasure is achieved, and in what sense. The real hedonist lives a rich, well-rounded life, cultivating his body into a figure of beauty and strength, and enjoying many indulgences – but not to such an excessive degree that they cause him to suffer. The fake hedonist does not think about his future at all, and is a slave to his habits. He has convinced himself that his habits are "the things he likes," that they are "fun," and so on, but he finds in them only a few fleeting seconds of pleasure before the hangover sets in, or the upset stomach, or any number of other dreadful feelings of exhaustion. He does not make any attempt to prevent or even postpone these consequences, but he does make desperate attempts to prevent himself from *thinking* about the consequences of his actions, by continuing to distract himself.

The remarkable thing is that the fake hedonist may very well consider himself to be free. But what is the fruit of his freedom? What freedom is he exercising? The freedom to live a disgustingly boring and tasteless life? What is the advantage of the exercise of this freedom? Is he, like a child, rejoicing in the fact that he is *not* being chastised for his "pleasures" by some parent or supervisor? He is surely being chastised by his own body and mind, every minute that he is not immersed in some distraction (and many of the minutes in which he is so immersed). And this chastising by one's own body is much harsher than the chastising of a parent, because it cannot be written off as the arbitrary judgment of someone else, someone "on the outside." Perhaps someone very strongly in denial could chalk up all of their self-inflicted difficulties to fate, or genetics, or some self-diagnosed amorphous disease brought on by random chance. A person in such a state of denial is in for a large number of unpleasant surprises, a large number of events of "random chance," if they do not learn to recognize the consequences of their own actions.

LIES

A life fueled by distractions is only emptiness. A life made up of only excuses is hollow and meaningless. A life that consists of the important questions being ignored, put off, put to the side, eternally saved for later – this life is inconsequential and serves no purpose. This life makes no contributions whatsoever to the world, except through coincidence or chance. Is this satisfactory? What red-blooded human being will find it satisfactory? Naturally, many people who wake up one day and find themselves living a life of lies will find this state to be very *un*satisfactory. But those who are cold, the fake hedonists, the people clinging to excuses and distractions, will not change their lives. Their desire is not to change their lives, but to complain, to hope that someone else will change their lives, and to fantasize about a better life – but never to work for it, never to change their habits. Yes, some do manage to change their habits in the end, but most do not. Most never bother, most remain content to voice their lack of contentment. They are the ones who hate their problems, but who do not truly wish for a solution, because that would require effort – they wish only to sustain their present equilibrium of encountering problems and voicing complaints.

These people lie to themselves, they deny themselves. They are worse than hypocrites: a hypocrite would do what they condemn others for, but these people do nothing, and condemn the world. They do not do what they want, and they berate the world for not presenting them with what they want on a silver platter. The old adage, "If you want something done right, you have to do it yourself," comes to mind; I prefer to say, "If you want something done *at all*, you have to do it yourself." A person's desires are their character, and to leave these desires as mere fantasy, to never make them real, is to lack character, to lack integrity, and ultimately to lack existence as a human being.

Imagine a person in a prison cell who constantly dreams of escape. This person concocts elaborate fantasies of life on the outside, of how they would be a model human being, of how they would create great works of art, or at least have a job doing meaningful work, and how they would keep their house, how they would find a spouse and raise their children, and so on. The only catch is that they have to leave the prison cell to do it. But imagine that this person holds the key to their own cell, *knows that they have it*, and simply ignores this fact, saying to themselves that they are trapped (or, equally bad, not saying it aloud, but constantly acting as if this is the case), and continuing to merely fantasize. What kind of cruel self-deprecating joke is this? Could there be a greater waste of potential? How many people confine themselves to their houses or apartments, and live this very same life?

And the above also applies, in a less literal sense, to certain people who are "outgoing." I put that word in quotation marks because it's very possible for a person to appear outgoing, vivacious, extraverted, while really only putting up a façade, an act, hiding their true personality, their true desires. How many people put up such acts, such walls obscuring their true character, for some form of social status that they have fooled themselves into thinking they must maintain? Is it worth it to sacrifice one's honesty, one's self-expression, for something so ethereal?

MISERABLE EASE

Here's another fundamental motivation to consider, a practically universal one: the desire to make life easier. The image of "the easy life" pervades culture – the life of the old-money aristocrat, the retired entrepreneur or celebrity, the lottery winner. The image is of a person who has all of the resources they need to sustain their lifestyle for as long as they live, and consequently, who does not have to work a job. Work is an annoyance; it might be physically taxing or mentally tedious, or both. It is a human instinct to want to avoid doing unnecessary work, but some people try to go further, and avoid work altogether. This behavior is typical of the fake hedonist, the cold person, who frames work as a negative experience universally, who is afraid of the notion that some kind of deliberate effort might be necessary to get what they want, and who subsequently tells themselves that "what they want" is whatever can be acquired with no effort (or, better yet, what *ought to* be available with no effort; with this, they have fuel for additional complaints).

Imagine a person who wins the lottery and decides to, in the vein of the (pre-hypnosis) main character from *Office Space,* do nothing but sit and watch TV all day, every day. This person no longer needs to work a salaried job, which is a lot of work alleviated already; but it is not yet zero work. The lottery winner hires a driver and a butler, and never does anything if they can pay someone else to do it. No more doing the dishes, mowing the lawn, washing the car, vacuuming, cooking, etc. But this is still not zero work. Perhaps this person buys a mobility scooter or an electric wheelchair because, even though they can walk, they don't want to if they can avoid it. Perhaps suspicious bottles and cans start appearing in this person's designated television-watching room, with an expectation that they will be removed by the cleaning staff. Perhaps this person hires a maid to feed them at the dinner table, simply because it's within their budget.

It is not a healthy desire to try to eliminate work altogether. I've heard that in nursing homes, the staff are often specifically instructed *not* to help the elderly residents with whatever aspects of self-care they can still perform themselves, because this would be degrading to them, to remove their last vestiges of independent activity. Additionally, anyone who has ever been unemployed should know all too well that it's not a pleasant experience, even if you are able to mooch off of somebody else. To be dependent on somebody else is unpleasant because you're in their pocket, at their mercy, restricted by their schedule and lifestyle. And depending on the provider's personality, you may even find yourself on their leash. Even in the cases where the provider is kind, boredom sets in easily, a boredom so pervasive that it will even gnaw through the infinite distractions offered by a reliable Internet connection. However "easy" it might be, however much one's quantity of work to do in life has been lessened, it won't matter. It will only become more obvious that easiness does not imply happiness.

Those who are too committed to not committing themselves to anything will also run into the issue of not doing anything with their lives. If you are not working, then you are not working to improve your life. If you are not doing anything, then you are not doing what you want. As tempting as it might be to try to imitate the image of the rich person and bring one's life closer to a state of "doing no work," this essentially amounts to "doing nothing," which is not a desirable way to live on general principle. One reason for this is illustrated by the stereotypical situation where a person is asked something like "Tell me about yourself," or "So, have any plans for this weekend?" and has difficulty coming up with an answer. These are difficult questions for a person who is not really doing anything with their life, and who is simultaneously conscientious enough that they consider the distractions that they actually fill their time with too embarrassing to reveal. One option is lying, but the conscientious person doesn't want to lie either. The real solution is obvious: the person should develop some actual interests and do something with their time, so that they can both give a good answer to such questions and have this answer be the truth – contrary to the temptation to try to do as little as possible. Strange though it might sound, there are plenty of people who will choose, every time this situation occurs, to tell some half-hearted lie or self-deprecating joke and wait for the uncomfortable social situation to pass by; and they will then feel guilty about living an empty life, turn to the very distractions they don't want to admit they occupy all their time with, and feel even guiltier until they manage to become completely engrossed in their diversion of choice. That being said, if a situation like this occurs often enough, it may not be so easy to ignore. Some people therefore throw the baby out instead of the bathwater, and try to avoid social events so that they don't need to risk a situation that might make them confront the plain and simple reality of their lifestyle.

This idea of work, this framing of it as something universally undesirable, is nonsense to anybody who takes the time to think about what a life without *any* work would actually look like. How might a person wind up with this misguided idea stuck in their head? It might have come about due to some kind of childhood experience – perhaps due to a normal event misinterpreted (e.g., a person had responsible parents who made this person do chores as a child, and this person resented the parents for that, never understanding that helping around the house made things better for everyone) or perhaps due to actual trauma (e.g., a person had abusive parents who would make them do chores, and then invariably chastise and beat them for "failing" regardless of the quality of their work). Or perhaps a person once led a very busy life, and clung tightly to every bit of relaxation they could get; and then their life became not so busy, but they still keep trying to pursue the maximal amount of "relaxation." Such a person as this will find out pretty quickly that too much of a "relaxing" activity will cease to be relaxing; a "rewarding" condition is only rewarding if there also exists, in recent memory, a "non-rewarding" condition against which it can be contrasted. Either way, for practical purposes, one must either make a deliberate effort to grow as a person and understand that work actually can be desirable, or else suffer the consequences of eternally doing nothing, of living a pointless life. To wish to do no work, to have no desire to work for the sake of positive, deliberate improvement, is the very opposite of wishing for a meaningful Answer to the Question. To answer the Question is to determine exactly what one wants in life, and how to achieve it – decisive action requires work, and therefore, a person who has no intention of working has no intention of answering the Question.

NEGATIVE DESIRES

Several pertinent "easing" or "lessening" desires have an interesting common element. The desire to think in simple terms; the desire to be dependent; the desire to know that one is backed by a power *separate* from oneself; the desire to sleep constantly; the desire to be controlled; the desire to have a clear and simple direction in life.

These are all negative desires. They all have the common theme of a desire to make one's life easier, less complex, simpler, requiring fewer responsibilities. The desire to NOT think in complex or nuanced terms; the desire to NOT be independent; the desire to NOT hold responsibility for power oneself, and simultaneously to NOT ever go against power held by someone else; the desire to NOT be awake and active; the desire to NOT have freedom; the desire to NOT have to make careful decisions and continually think about and revise one's judgments about one's direction in life.

If each of the above desires is taken to its ultimate form, its most extreme conclusion, a singular result emerges. The desire to not have ANY thoughts; the desire to not have ANY independent existence; the desire to not have ANY power for oneself, and to not have ANY ability to go against any other power; to not have ANY wakefulness, awareness, or activity; to not have ANY freedom; to not have the ability to make ANY judgments.

The desire for death emerges, death as the ultimate relief. Some might try to frame all of the above desires, even in their elementary form, as manifestations of a subconscious desire to die; but that might be an overly reductive way of looking at things. It is satisfactory, at least, to say that these desires and the desire to die can occur for similar reasons – and that one should be very careful not to cling too closely to these desires, one should not carry them too far, or else one's life will start to resemble death, for the realization of these desires may bring a person closer to death. The very dependent person becomes a parasite, unable to live without a host; the very subservient person becomes ineffectual and is only thrown about by life.

The similarity between these desires and the desire to die is most prominent when one or more of these desires is part of a person's fundamental conception of their self – in other cases, it is less likely the case that a desire in this category is truly death-oriented. For instance, imagine a person who dreams of a utopia where no one has to work, and all labor required for the functioning of civilization is done by machines. While this person is wishing to be "dependent" on the labor-machines as well as the systems that fund their room and board, that does not mean this person is of a fundamentally "dependent" character. Perhaps this person is an artist who wants the freedom to produce their art or music without being constrained by the issues which naturally arise in today's familiar economic environment. These would be issues of budget, scheduling, and mental focus, issues that could be hypothetically avoided in a different world. In contrast, it's not at all uncommon to find people who are much more literally "dependent," having dependence as a fundamental aspect of their character, and of their perception of themselves – dependent on other people, dependent on drugs, dependent on such-and-such means of entertainment, whatever the case may be. Now, try to imagine the perspective of those who perceive themselves as fundamentally dependent, who do not conceive of themselves as independent and capable beings – do they consider themselves to be truly alive? Or is something missing?

FEAR OF SUCCESS

Nobody can come to proper terms with the Question, the ultimate evaluation of success or failure, if they are afraid of success. While few people would insult themselves by consciously considering themselves to be "afraid of success," there are indeed people who fear it, and they can be detected by their characteristic actions.

There are several fears that factor into the fear of success. None of these fears are rational; a person living with any one of them ought to change their perspective if they intend to deal with the Question effectively. First is the *de facto* fear of success that is essentially equivalent to a fear of work, discussed just above. Second is the general fear of change, the fear of breaking one's equilibrium and having life be different in general. Third is the related fear of the responsibilities of success, of one's life becoming more difficult or ending up under tighter scrutiny after one has achieved something significant. Fourth is the more subtle dread of changing one's life "for the better" – only to have that change be utterly meaningless. The psychology and signs of living with the first and second fears have already been discussed. The third one is a sort of misdirected fear: the only conditions in which success would lead to a tangibly worse overall outcome are situations involving abusive employers or family members, and whoever lives in these conditions should redirect their fear away from the prospect of personal success and toward their abusers; and hopefully, acknowledging the true threat in this way, they can do something about it. If this isn't the case, then a person who refuses to work toward their goals, for fear of life becoming more difficult as a result, can only be called lazy. What is there to say about a person who wants to become a lawyer, but doesn't pursue the career because it would involve too much difficult studying? It's not meaningful to say that they really *want* to become a lawyer, since they don't want to do what becoming a lawyer entails.

It is the fourth fear that is especially interesting, suggesting a far greater threat than a break of equilibrium: it is the fear that one's hopes and dreams are all for nothing, that one will feel just as unsatisfied with life once they have done all of the "satisfying things" they imagine themselves doing. Surely, the hesitant mind imagines, it's better to feel the pleasure of fantasizing about success than to risk discovering that success brings no pleasure whatsoever! Two birds in the bush are worth one in the hand, after all. Surely, it's better to have hopes and dreams existing in the mind, though eternally unfulfilled, than to have one's very *concept* of hopes and dreams shattered by their actual execution! What is more frightening a prospect than the fantastic concept of success being utterly destroyed by an anticlimax of real success? What could be worse than knowing, through direct experience, that a satisfying success cannot be achieved?

This subtle fear can be extremely powerful, even when it only lurks in the subconscious mind, out of the reach of conscious criticism. If it can be consciously analyzed, though, a critical flaw appears. Namely, the mindset of this fear only appeals to people who have forgotten, or who choose to ignore, actual instances of satisfaction in life. Even the most rudimentary form of successful work should yield satisfaction. Even something as simple as cleaning one's house, exercising, or doing a good job on a task at school or at work, should be satisfying to some degree. This should be sufficient reason to believe that more ambitious projects (that is, ambitious in regards to what one truly wants) should yield greater satisfaction, and that the building of healthy life habits (i.e., the regular achievement of simple successes) should help to keep a person in a more generally satisfied state of mind – or at least prevent the opposite of satisfaction, shame, from building up excessively. These simple facts of life are proof positive that the fear is illegitimate, not an actual reason to remain complacent with an inadequate life. To a person struggling with doubts of this type, consider also the idea's origin; and consider it carefully, really try to isolate the root of it. If someone were to convey this idea to you in the form of a piece of advice, telling you, "Do not work to achieve this thing, because you will feel no better for having done it, and you will be worse off for having wasted your time" – what kind of a person is this? Is this someone with your best interests in mind? Is this someone who wants you to achieve what you want, or is it someone who wants you to do nothing, merely misery seeking company? On the other hand, there is another important possibility – if there is some kind of tangible evidence that the path laid out before you in life will lead to dissatisfaction, and especially if your efforts to move down that path have not brought you even a small amount of happiness, perhaps this path is simply not what you want. Perhaps you have fooled yourself into thinking that this thing is what you want, based on some kind of pressure from your peers, family, or media, and it's not really the path to a life you would love. This will be explored further in Part IV.

It's obvious that none of these items stand up to scrutiny, once exposed for what they are; the only defenses of them are poor coping mechanisms for a person who does not wish to acknowledge the Question and actually evaluate their life. And without evaluating one's life, one cannot improve it. These are insincere coping mechanisms too, because they effectively defend the sentiment "I am afraid of success," a sentiment too embarrassing for anyone to earnestly say, even to themselves. To succumb to these inclinations is to do nothing, to remain inanimate, to bring one's life closer to death. Beware of fearful attitudes such as this. From fears like this, a hatred of life can emerge. If a person fears success and justifies failure, it's not too far a leap to consider an utterly failed life justified, and to resent and hate the successful. And from this, a person might even start to develop stranger ideas still, perhaps thinking that being weak is strictly better than being strong, or that being disabled or diseased is strictly better than being healthy. How many resentful people secretly hold such opinions, as half-baked justifications for their own failures?

AXIOM

The rejection of the Question is not always outright – it can also be ignored implicitly. An important strategy of this type is the assumption that the Question has already been answered, to assume that there exists a universal answer for every person: this would be a "no" answer to suicide, of course, an answer in favor of life. The person advocating such a thing is often playing the part of the faithful humanitarian, the person with absolute confidence in the value of every human being. The belief expressed by this kind of person is the belief that every human being's life is valuable and meaningful, and that even the worst person can have a change of heart and become virtuous. This axiomatic perspective utterly refuses to admit any argument that suicide is an option, dodging the issue by attempting to supersede it.

The first flaw with this perspective is, obviously, the axiomatic nature of it. It can't be used to convince a person who doesn't *already* believe in that sort of thing on the level of axiom, just as a religious person can't convince an atheist to convert by explaining that the sacred texts are infallible. This also means that, in a moment of crisis, one cannot use it to convince *oneself* not to commit suicide. It's dangerous to hold an axiomatic position like this, since, in the end, the belief that suicide is universally wrong (as it is held by this person) is not based on some kind of evidence or even a theoretical argument, but only a belief about human nature; the advocate may make arguments, but they all hinge on this belief, this central assumption. Beliefs can come and go very rapidly – what happens if some painful revelation should call this belief into question? What if the emotional inclination to escape from suffering begins to outweigh the inclination to cling to this axiomatic belief? Disaster looms. The belief only remains relevant while the individual is in a cheerful enough state of mind that they have little interest in actually committing suicide. If a person's "reason to live" is something as flimsy as this belief, then that reason to live will quickly be shattered by a period of great enough stress, a time during which life seems torturous, a time during which this "belief" is no longer in the forefront of one's mind – when it is eclipsed by unbearable pain.

The second flaw is that the theory itself is questionable. Even outside the special cases of martyrdom and euthanasia, the optimistic idea that no human being's life is worth destroying is only true in a limited sense. It's true in the sense that every human being has potential for improvement, and that potential for improvement is strictly better than no potential for improvement whatsoever (the condition of the dead). However, this potential value is only potential – not actual. It's a mistake to say something like "every human being's life *is* valuable" given how many people exist who live lives of absolutely no value, or worse, who live destructive lives, having essentially negative value. I am not talking about flawed people, people with negative traits but also some redeeming factors; I mean those with no redeeming factors whatsoever. There are people like this. In addition to the overtly destructive and psychopathic, there are rotten people, who do not overtly harm others (though they would like to, if they felt they could get away with it), but who live full of resentment and hatred for the world around them, knowingly playing the part of the parasite, taking everything that they can and giving as little as possible back. In between and around these are various shades of abusers, bullies, cheaters, and manipulators. While any person of this description could technically stop at any time, while any such person has the *potential* to change in the future, such a change is only speculation as of the present. It is inaccurate to say that they *are* valuable – looking at things as they are in the present, these kinds of people hold negative value. Granted, there certainly exist people who do both significant good and significant evil in one lifetime, and these cases can be difficult to judge in an overall sense; but there are some whose lives are far less difficult to judge, those whose actions are overwhelmingly on the side of evil. And by "evil," I mean not just badness, but actual malevolence; not merely crimes of negligence or even callous opportunism (let alone crimes truly committed out of desperation), but the deliberate infliction of harm onto other people for no reason other than sport. Such monsters do exist, and a sane person observing one will wonder: "How could a human being become something like this?" The notion that such a person may one day have a change of heart and start bringing positive value to the world, suddenly behaving antithetically to their entire past, is only speculation. The thought that such a person's suicide would bring more harm than gain is dubious.

Of course, a person monstrous enough to qualify as this type will not likely be conscientious enough to consider their suicide to be a morally correct action. The example is only shown to illustrate that, in principle, the potential to have value does not equate to value. As another way of describing this point: to try to dodge the Question by citing some wholesome maxim like "everyone's life has value" is to ignore the fact that the default value of a life is zero. It is only one's actions that can imbue one's life with value. The potential for action, the ability to do something valuable, does not imply value, strictly speaking – it is only potential. Every life is potentially valuable, yes – but unless that value is produced, the actual value of the life is zero, or perhaps less than zero. To insist otherwise is typical of those who cling to an axiomatic non-answer to the Question.

Note, by the way, an interesting fact about the axiomatic belief. It's flimsy, not for a logical reason, but for a practical reason. The statement "having potential is better than dying and having no potential" is completely sound – there's hardly a person out there who would deny it. But mere logical soundness is not enough. Remember: an argument will not convince the suicidal person to live simply because it is logical – because the suicidal person does not care. Simultaneously, an illogical argument will also fail to convince the suicidal person, whose mind is filled with doubt, and whose weary soul constantly searches for justifications for suicide, and who will be quick to recognize and disregard unsound arguments that favor life. Only something both convincing and logically sound will be satisfactory to address the Question – everything else must be discarded.

As a last resort, one might be tempted to say that it is the moments of crisis that are the real issue, that the moments of intense suffering, which will throw a person out of equilibrium and make suicide appear a more attractive option, are "abnormal;" or one might naïvely declare that *nothing* should ever be considered a serious threat to one's faith in life. But it is a mistake bordering on delusion to write such critical mental experiences off as if they were merely a "foreign" phenomenon, like an illness, or worse, to imagine that they will never happen. Some people are lucky enough that these periods of intense suffering occur infrequently – perhaps so infrequently that one imagines that no further ones will ever occur. But no one is exempt from suffering, especially not those who live lives fueled by excuses. And arguments of the axiomatic sort are excuses – excuses to continue along the familiar equilibrium of life, and to not have to bother with the hassle of dying. Suffering is unavoidable, and in circumstances that would cause a healthy person to suffer, suffering is a healthy response.

SPITE

A somewhat different form of the axiomatic approach is the idea of continuing to live out of spite. This is the person who says, "I have to keep living, to prove wrong all those who say I can't make it in life, to prove wrong everyone who ever said I was too weak." This "I have to" concept is what makes the argument axiomatic – this thing that the person "has to do" is considered, undeniably, without question, a satisfactory reason for living. This runs directly into the problems with axiomatic reasoning already mentioned.

The argument from spite is notable, though, because it's a totally different type of statement which is considered to be axiomatically true. It doesn't come from an attitude of universal positivity or humanitarianism or anything like that – it's a more personal, individual desire, smacking of a willingness to be contrary to others, to prove one's superiority to others' expectations. This doesn't make it any stronger of an argument in a technical sense, but it does suggest that the person in question has a desire to express what you might call their personal power, as an individual. The desire to exert power onto the world, laughing in the face of others' expectations, does actually have practical utility when it comes to developing an Answer to the Question; this will be explored in Part IV. Perhaps, odd though it might sound, the person who mentally justifies their life through spite is actually closer to reaching an appropriate perspective than the one who takes the purely humanitarian approach.

The argument from spite is, at best, a stepping stone toward stronger arguments; in addition to the problem of being axiomatic, it also has a unique flaw. Just as it's possible for a person's comfort with life to go away, and thus knock the bottom out of their confidence in the inherent goodness of life, it's possible for a person's emotional incentives towards spite to simply go away at some point. The premise is that people are judging you, saying that you're not good enough, and that you have to prove these people wrong. But what if these people are removed from your life? What if you move far away from these people, or if they stop caring about you and they move on to bullying someone else? Or, better yet, what if you change your life for the better, and they stop viewing you so negatively, and they no longer feel the need to act harsh towards you? The emotional inclination towards spite disappears. The motivating idea of "I have to prove them wrong" becomes irrelevant if there is no "them" to antagonize you; if this sensation of being antagonized goes away, will you simply lapse into inaction? Or will you place yourself into antagonistic situations with other people, so that you have a villain to rebel against? Spitefulness is not a good personality trait to retain in the long term.

RATIONALIZING INACTION

"No matter what a person does, life is still worth living." Once a person has ingrained in their mind this axiomatic idea, it's very easy to rationalize inaction. The lazy person, the cold or superficial person who only wants to remain distracted, will use the very positive-sounding phrase "life is worth living, no matter what" as a rationalization to maintain an equilibrium with no purpose, no prospects of moving to some better equilibrium, some better state of life. Their objective, if it can even be called that, is only to experience a continuous stream of distractions, momentary whims, new activities every minute, anything to keep the mind occupied and entertained. They act as if, and perhaps even think that, this wholesome-sounding phrase not only forgives all faults, but renders all concept of fault or inadequacy irrelevant.

This is yet another reason why the axiomatic approach is not a legitimate answer to the Question: the axiom, in this case, is not used to argue a justification for life, or even as a reason to perform any particular action, but merely as an excuse to say that one's present condition in life is adequate. It is not an incentive to do something with one's life, it is not a purpose or an expression of one's will or anything like that, but only an excuse to continue doing nothing.

One byproduct of this rationalization of inaction would be the lowering of one's standards for oneself until they are already satisfied by the present equilibrium. If a person wants to do certain things (e.g., exercise, eat healthy, pay the bills on time, clean themselves and their surroundings) but never does them, they could try to rationalize that kind of inaction by saying to themselves, if not an overt axiomatic statement of life being undeniably worth living, something like "I don't really need to, I'm living such a good life already that doing something like that would be pushing myself too far, and after all, I wouldn't want to overexert myself..." and so on. Even someone obese and sedentary might muster up the gall to make this kind of statement, as if they're living life on the edge. A person very deeply invested in this rationalization of inaction could even go to further extremes, even *actively chastising* people for making healthy decisions, saying sarcastic things like "What, do you want to live forever?" Or perhaps something more ideological, along the lines of "Great people are born great, and you're not one of them, so it's pathetic and futile to even try to become great." This is the crabs-in-a-bucket mentality, the mentality of the person who wants to drag others down to their level. The fact that some people can carry this mentality to the point of delusion is a testament to the power of the human mind to rationalize whatever dumb ideas it comes up with. That said, there are some easily-manipulated people who would take such claims seriously, people who might actually be convinced that trying to improve themselves is a bad thing, or an exercise in futility, *categorically*. Young and impressionable people are at higher risk of becoming the victims of this sort of general demoralization. Here are a couple of questions to consider when faced with someone trying to convince you of something like that: First, if you shouldn't try to improve yourself, what exactly should you be doing instead? Staying the same, or making your life worse? Second, is "don't even try" the kind of advice that is given by a person who knows what they're talking about, someone who's a winner, a success? Or is it more likely that the person giving this "advice" is only a loser, a failure, trying to drag others down?

Now, let's describe the inactive state of equilibrium which is being rationalized here. It's a state that the person in question undoubtedly finds unpleasant or even intolerable, and which this person is likely to constantly complain about, to themselves if not to others. But nonetheless, the equilibrium is still rationalized and maintained. This behavior, when observed plainly for what it is, seems absurd and difficult to explain. It's probably most accurate to say that people cling to this kind of equilibrium because they find a sort of comfort in living that way, maintaining that condition. Note that this is not "comfort" in the sense of physical comfort or even mental tranquility, but a more primitive form of comfort, the comfort of having life continue according to the same understood pattern day after day. Even if this pattern involves continuous suffering, people are often surprisingly willing to tolerate the devil that they know and expect. If they imagine that their way of life can never change, that their suffering is unavoidable, then the intolerable can become tolerable, and their excessive suffering simply becomes "another part of life," just something to get used to. If feeling bad is the norm, a person can, with practice, warp their feelings and perceptions so much that it starts to feel good to feel bad. That is, until the stress from this suffering starts wearing their sanity thin. The excuse of "I can't avoid it, so I may as well get used to it" will not fool a person forever, if the thing in question is in fact avoidable. For truly unavoidable things, on the other hand, such as incurable medical conditions, this ability to adapt has real utility in helping people to function through difficult circumstances.

It's sometimes enjoyable to smugly say to yourself, "Shall I work on what I want today? No, I think I will take a break." But even when taking breaks, you should have a plan. The part of the mind that likes repeating the same decision might latch onto the fact that a break occurred yesterday, and tempt you to take another break today. "It was okay to do this yesterday, so it should also be okay today." How many break days will be enough? How many things left undone will remain undone, how far will the unfinished business pile up? Will even ordinary items, such as diet and hygiene, also become subject to the break, as the level of effort is brought lower and lower? How low is low enough? How much lower would you like to get before you decide to recover? Technically, a person could remain in a very low such state indefinitely, constantly in denial; but that would mean suffering indefinitely, and probably suffering an increasing amount over time. Even given the ability of the human brain to rationalize all sorts of ridiculous behaviors, it would take a very warped mind to entrench itself in a permanent state of denial.

The thought comes to mind of the sort of disturbed person whose living conditions, which they consider "normal," make up the disgusting horror stories of paramedics and firemen.

One could characterize the desire to remain in equilibrium as a desire to have to think as little as possible, to avoid the possibility of confronting new ideas, to avoid having a larger number of "things to think about," that is, responsibilities. While there is a practical limit to the number of things a person can regularly think about, using this as an excuse to do as little as possible with one's life is, to put it lightly, impractical.

Incidentally, it is also very possible for a person to behave in this manner without having "life is universally worth living" consciously in mind. If a person only holds this belief subconsciously, perhaps not knowing exactly what it is that they're holding, they might perform actions like this for reasons they themselves don't entirely understand. This phenomenon will be discussed in a wider context in Part III, in the section "Limbo of Belief."

NORMAL PEOPLE

One way of rationalizing inaction is by considering oneself "just a normal person." A person looks at himself and observes that he is not superintelligent, nor rich, nor famous, and that fate has not yet dealt a miraculous boon to him, and he concludes that he is "just a normal person," fundamentally separate from the great leaders and great artists and great scientists of the world. The fallacy here is the insistence that a person's life remains the same forever, that because a person is not presently living an important life, that this person will never live an important life. This fixed belief, that great success is entirely off the table, is a convenient excuse for those who are, consciously or subconsciously, trying to avoid putting effort into their lives. It reflects the urge to equilibrium discussed before, the urge to keep everything the same, and the fear of change, even the fear of success.

When conceptualizing oneself as a "normal person," one's options for life are quickly bound by what one considers society's expectations of "normal people" to be. Do normal people have hopes and dreams, beyond reaching a medium-level managerial position on the corporate ladder, or beyond finally paying off one's mortgage and becoming debt-free? Hardly. To wish to become a great artist is not normal – how many people with a strong interest in art refuse their passions because they don't want to be perceived as abnormal? Some people grow up being told that wanting to work a blue-collar job is abnormal, that one instead has to go to college and work in an office – how many people would be satisfied with a career working with their hands, who instead resign themselves to tediously working on a keyboard in a cubicle, slowly paying off an overbearing student loan?

A person can obstruct themselves from what they want, and can push themselves into what they don't want, if they choose to consider "being normal" as a virtue, or worse, an imperative. Peer pressure is a powerful thing – even more so in the Information Age, where a person can be pressured by peer groups that they aren't even a part of, just by observing enough people communicating such-and-such idea on the Internet. In spite of the fact that today's tolerant society will be happy to tell you, over and over again, in every piece of media from movies to children's picture books to corporate slogans, that "it's okay to be different," and in spite of the fact that there is a wider berth for diverse means of self-expression than ever (at least, in those nations that have freedom of speech), the pervasive concept of "normal" emerges in culture anyway, and fear of being different persists. Acting from that fear, rather than acting on one's actual desires, is poison. It is an ugly thing to cling to social pressures and to try to act out the imagined character of "the normal person," the person with no aspirations or interests beyond the most pedestrian and popular, the person whose favorite movie is the one they most recently saw, the person who would do absolutely nothing but sit at home and watch TV if they won the lottery, etc.

"The normal person" is also not something that anybody really wants to be, deep down. Most people want to be normal in a number of ways, ways that are beneficial to their maintenance of a healthy equilibrium and a healthy method of interaction with the world. But nobody wants to be totally ordinary, because to be totally ordinary is to never be extraordinary. Even the very introverted person, who is happy to navigate most of life without fanfare, has an actual individual personality which they would like to express in some fashion, which they would like to share with others given the opportunity. To be normal in every way is to be a nobody.

OBSESSION OVER THE PAST

Another self-constraining behavior is the conceptualization of oneself as some sort of victim or perpetually impotent person based on obsession with some past event, or some pre-existing circumstance. Conceptualization of self as victim does not necessarily occur in as literal a sense as the case of the "normal person" – it's not often that a person will literally think to themselves, "I'm a victim, I'm hopelessly disadvantaged, and there's nothing I can do about it but complain." This might happen occasionally, but more often, the conceptualization will be *de facto* expressed through inaction, a negative outlook on the outside world, and a particular habit of brooding over the past.

It's the excessive focus on the past that makes this behavior special; the injuries or faults or failures of the past are used as an excuse to maintain an equilibrium of inaction in the present, and thoughts of such things constantly occupy the person's mind. Here, the pattern of thinking is a constant reflection of those past events, and a constant repetition of the same line of reasoning, "explaining" why the events of the past led to the person being a failure in the present. While it does make sense to want to investigate past events in order to figure out what led to an unfavorable present, this line of reasoning becomes troublesome when it takes a sharp turn and abruptly concludes with something like "therefore, I am destined to fail in all my efforts and shouldn't even bother trying." The half-baked penultimate step could be something along the lines of "I have constantly failed in all my previous efforts," or "I am being sabotaged and oppressed by an insurmountable adversary," or some other such dreary sentiment, which sometimes might even be true. But, directly after this, the additional logical step required to conclude "don't even try" – where is it exactly? It doesn't exist. The step is skipped; the argument is incomplete. This "line of reasoning" is only a thinly disguised rationalization of inaction. It only exists so that the person can consider their subpar life to be adequate, or "the best I can do given the circumstances," justified by a sequence of words said to oneself in a fashion vaguely resembling a logical argument. Looking carefully at such a line of reasoning, this is actually pretty obvious – in fact, a person who is exemplifying this very behavior might hear this explanation and agree. They may even have reflected on the state of their life and come up with the same conclusion on their own (it is, again, quite obvious). Unfortunately, just because this is a fact doesn't mean that it's convincing. Most people, upon discovering a fact like this about their own behavior, are likely to briefly feel sorry for themselves, go out and distract themselves somehow, and proceed to do absolutely nothing about their own self-admitted excuse-making. Is it that difficult to simply be honest with yourself?

ANTIDEPRESSANTS

As much trust as we would like to have in our fellow human beings, and loathe though we may be to accuse our mental health patients of lying, the fact remains that antidepressants can be acquired under illegitimate pretenses and be abused. There are those who seek a high, and there are those who seek to escape from negative emotion – even those negative emotions which are warranted. Attempting to forcibly tear one's own mental focus away from issues that warrant negative emotion is one more way to try to avoid the Question.

It's tempting to imagine a cure for unhappiness. A naïve person hears about antidepressants and imagines that their own negative emotion – which they say to themselves is absolutely unwarranted, unusual, a manifestation of some disease of the brain – can finally be disposed of. Some people who assess themselves in this way are correct, they have identified a real problem in their own mind. Others are incorrect, in denial, wishing to run away from problems that they could defeat if they tried, maybe even easily. But how to tell the difference? How to tell when medicine is the correct choice, and when it is not, when therapy and lifestyle adjustments are enough? This determination is the task of both the psychologist and the patient. The patient must be honest to themselves and to their healthcare providers in order to get the best results, and this can be a surprisingly large obstacle; it is very easy to be dishonest to both parties.

It's obvious that negative emotion has utility, and that lying to oneself, remaining in denial about the nature of negative emotion, will have tangible consequences. Perhaps a person constantly feels bad because they are regularly being abused or bullied, but for some reason they refuse to consciously admit to themselves that this abuse is happening. If they do not admit this to themselves or to their doctor, and if they should be prescribed a drug which eliminates this negative emotion, what happens? A person continues being abused but does not feel so bad about it? Is this an improvement? Or suppose that a person lives a squalid, self-destructive lifestyle, constantly inflicting unnecessary problems onto themselves and constantly failing to do elementary things that they absolutely have the power to do, and then feeling guilty about it all the time. If this guilt is removed by way of medicine, will this person simply feel good about living a terrible life? Is this a solution?

This is not to suggest discarding antidepressants (and anti-anxiety drugs, etc.) entirely, of course. Even in the above-mentioned scenarios, a healthy and productive path forward might involve the use of medication, maybe even for a long period. What these examples are meant to illustrate is the importance of being realistic and honest about one's problems in life. The attitude of the patient, walking into a psychologist's office, should not simply be seeking out a quick-and-easy fix; it should be to communicate honestly, acknowledge and understand the problems in their life, and work together to prepare a plan for the future, a path forward. The proper attitude therefore includes a certain skepticism, a skepticism of the idealistic notion of "A drug can simply cure me of all my problems." This fantasy might be so tantalizing that it could tempt a person to lie to their doctor in order to make themselves eligible for a certain kind of drug. It might also tempt a person to stay on a drug that is not working, or which is having serious side effects, or which is outrageously expensive, in the hope that it will eventually make everything better if they just stick to this new status quo long enough. Similarly important is the skepticism of the idea that "Whatever a doctor tells me is correct." Doctors, psychologists, psychiatrists, and so on can be wrong, and the first item they suggest is not always the right one – it might just be that which seems to work for the most people in (what they believe to be) the patient's situation. It is the authority of the patient to be able to say "Look, Doctor, this treatment just isn't working," or "I'm not sure that I want to try this kind of treatment, can we try such-and-such first," or "I'm not feeling like we're making progress, I'm going to try a different doctor." A willingness to say these things, should they become necessary, is part of being honest, a part of open communication. Openness means both an openness to try different things and an openness to admit when something's not working; an openness to say yes and an openness to say no.

ASSUMING THE CONCLUSION

The last technique of non-answering is assuming the desirable conclusion, assuming that the answer to the Question is no, that suicide is not the right choice, and working backwards from there to rationalize (essentially, to invent or improvise) reasons why it's wrong. This tactic doesn't sound unreasonable at first, and in fact, it is closely related to a legitimate method of scoping out potential Answers to the Question. The critical difference is that while this technique can be employed as part of the long, deliberate, and thorough process of developing an Answer (which will be discussed in Part IV), it loses its value if the process is halted halfway. A person can come up with a rationalization that sounds acceptable in-the-moment and simply stop there, assume that the Question has been answered to a satisfactory degree, and then sink back into their present equilibrium, just as if they had adopted the axiomatic approach. Indeed, it's practically identical to the axiomatic approach – a maxim is produced and treated as a totally sufficient proof that one's life is justified. The only difference is that the person has employed a half-baked "reasoning" process in order to generate this maxim (or, perhaps more likely than a concrete maxim, a vague thought, an abstract, unfinished concept, something that wouldn't stand up if subjected to actual scrutiny). Obviously, most readers won't be quick to call their own reasoning process "half-baked," so it's important to point out the warning signs that an argument of this type, which may seem "rational," is only the product of an incomplete process, and is not quite as sturdy as it appears.

What does this process look like? It starts when a person, in the throes of some existential dread, resorts to their survival instinct and says to themselves something like this: "I'm not going to kill myself, so I need to come up with a reason why." There's a mistake in here right off the bat, though not a huge one: assuming the conclusion, assuming that the desired result is correct, which is bad science. A more technically correct way of beginning the reasoning process would be something like: "Should I kill myself or not?" It's fair at this point to hold in the back of one's mind the rationally-conceived understanding that suicide is probably not a good idea – probably. The broader question "If there is a good reason to stay alive, what could it be?" can always be brought up afterwards. Anyway, that first mistake is more or less excusable. After acknowledging the Question, the person will go through various commonplace rationalizations for life, from various perspectives. "Murder is wrong, so I shouldn't murder myself." "Even a bad life is better than no life, because a bad life can be improved." "My dog wouldn't know where I went." Eventually, with their survival instinct earnestly looking for a good reason to live, the person selects something that sounds good, says to themselves "That'll work," and stops the reasoning process there. This is the more severe problem. It's only a short-term solution, it's not a holistic perspective toward one's own life. It suffers, in practice, all the same flaws as the axiomatic approach, but with a slightly more convincing disguise; it suggests that one has "solved the problem," that one has reasoned through it, proved their case. But the case is far from rock-solid; it is only solid enough to protect against a few small flickers of the suicidal urge at a time. When the urge becomes stronger, more overbearing, and the mind begins to incessantly doubt and doubt, meticulously looking for cracks in the existing arguments for life, the defense will not stand up.

A relevant item to note here is that rationalization is not at all a rational process. A person can rationalize anything, from the indulgence of momentary whims to the maintenance of a brutal ideological stance, if they have fooled themselves into thinking that it's the "rational" thing to think. Attempting to merely rationalize a reason why suicide is wrong could absolutely be skewed by personal biases, especially the person's "intuitive" perceptions of life, assumptions about life which are not robustly researched and which are liable to be totally wrong. If a large enough revelation of the inaccuracy of one's assumptions about life should appear – what happens to the foundations of one's attitude towards death? For example, a person might appeal to the virtuous nature of the human species as part of their rationalization of non-suicide – but what if this assumption about human nature is grossly misinformed, what if it is merely the product of a person who was coddled and sheltered in their youth, and who has not yet seen a real example of human cruelty in action? To have an assumption like this shattered, especially if it was the cornerstone of a person's rationalization of non-suicide, is to lose hope, to lose faith in humanity – it means the destruction of an overly idealistic image of the world. Losing this idealistic hope for the first time, much like contemplating suicide for the first time, is an essential step to becoming mentally mature. Occasionally, when an older person is struck with genuine tragedy for the first time in their otherwise comfortable life, they might react not merely emotionally but erratically, like a child throwing a tantrum; it creates a disturbing scene. Maybe a person has heard about acts of cruelty happening elsewhere, in foreign countries and foreign cities, and while this person is "aware" of cruelty in an academic sense, they have not seen it in person. They think to themselves, if only subconsciously, "it can't happen here, it can't happen to me" – so it's quite the revelation when they are mugged for the first time, or when they hold in their hands a disturbing letter from a stalker, or what have you.

FAITH

In promising times, when life seems to be teeming with good things to do, and when diverse paths toward a bright future seem to present themselves, a special temptation appears which deserves special mention. This temptation is faith. "There must exist a reason for me not to commit suicide, there must be a purpose that will make my life worth living. I know that one must exist, I just haven't found it yet. One day I will find it, and that will make the struggle of life that I am now facing worthwhile." This is not a detrimental sentiment for a person first scouting out possible Answers to the Question. It is a pleasant, optimistic sentiment that could certainly help a person through some difficult ordeal. But faith, like so many other optimistic sentiments, can be turned to poison. The poison appears when this faith is merely assumed, the sentimental attitude merely called to mind as a mental analgesic, and left at that. If there is no work being done to seek out this Answer, there is no reason to have faith in one's ability to find it. If a faith-espousing sentiment is brought to mind in times of trouble, but without any evidence that this faith is justified, how long will this faith last? A person can make self-affirming statements all day, every day – but after how many such statements, how many days and months and years of waiting in "faith," will pass before they finally decide to affirm themselves through action rather than words?

PART III: FAKE ANSWERS

ANSWER AS PURPOSE

There are methods of addressing the Question which are not so direct, which deal not with the question of suicide explicitly, but which concern a trait that any Answer to the Question must have: a proper Answer implies a purpose in life, a direction, a goal, a set of things that are important enough that death can be postponed until they have been achieved. If an Answer to the Question is a purpose in life, then to seek out a purpose in life is to seek out an Answer to the Question – even if suicide is not explicitly on the individual's mind during this seeking-out. The question of suicide is implicitly tied to any kind of self-evaluation, implicitly but intimately – and so, searching for a satisfactory answer to the question of suicide is equivalent to forging an identity, a character, a concept of the self which is worth striving for. Common phrases like "something to live for" or "what I'm living for" are identical to "a reason not to commit suicide."

Attacking the Question from the opposite side, so to speak, is perfectly legitimate, but not all methods of attacking in this manner are satisfactory. Just as Part II discussed inadequate methods of addressing the Question itself (the direct approach), this part will discuss inadequate methods of deciding on a purpose in life (the indirect approach). As such, suicide itself will not come up very often in this section.

A fundamental aspect of developing an Answer will be the construction of goals, goals for life, a conception of what you want to do before you die. Imagine, for instance, what you will reflect upon on your deathbed: what achievements will you reflect on? What creations do you want to leave behind? After you die, how will the world be different, better, for your having lived? If you intend to live a life that can be evaluated as having been worthwhile, then it's vitally important to understand the criteria of such an evaluation. If the goal is to perform actions that can be tangibly (that is, through evidence) evaluated as positive, then it immediately follows that this goal entails leaving a positive impact on the world. This doesn't mean that every person is obligated to be a world-shaking genius or a revolutionary; not everyone is capable of moving entire nations, but everyone is capable of moving *something*, changing *something* for the better. Even if you have some kind of severe disability and your greatest goal is to prove that you can be *something* more than a burden on the people around you, then by all means, have at it! Prove to everyone that you can contribute to society, even if your highest career aspiration is to be a janitor or a garbage man. Even that kind of person is far superior to the kind of educated, well-off person who does absolutely nothing, who has no aspirations and no purpose. The same goes for those with some humble creative aspiration or idea: contribute whatever creation you have the capacity for, even if that capacity is small – as long as it's real.

Now, an essential aspect of workable goals is that they have to be limited in scope. They have to be actually achievable and measurable; in other words, finite. Even if a person wants to do "as much work as they can" towards an ideal which would require a practically infinite amount of work to complete (e.g. abolishing war, ending world hunger), their specific goals, that which they intend to do within their own lifetime, will have to be finite. One way that goals can fail is if they are badly-conceptualized: for instance, a directionless person might, without making any particular plans, say to themselves that their goal in life is "to be a good person," and to just hope for the best. But this isn't a finite goal. How can someone measure their progress towards being a good person? Unless they formulate something more specific, the goal will be subject to an explosion of scope. A million issues emerge which a person could be called "good" for working to fix, but a single person can only handle so much.

The scope of one's goals has to be limited; this implies that the principles behind one's goals also have to be limited. In practice, whenever a person tries to formulate a set of principles for themselves, they will naturally start off with a simple set of rules, and in the best case, they will modify this set of rules as life goes on, adding more complexity and room for nuance as the demands of life require. But what if a person doesn't actually make their set of principles into anything more sophisticated than the set of simple rules that they came up with initially? What if they don't change their personal set of rules from that which they had in their head since, say, adolescence? Or, if they do change their set of rules to something else, what if it's just as simple and inadequate as the set of rules that they left behind? It's already been established that people can and often do go to great lengths to rationalize their present equilibrium, which includes their present set of principles. This can lead to a whole host of situations where people perceive the world according to a set of rules that are too simple for reality: rules of interpretation which cannot adequately model reality, and rules of action which cannot adequately navigate reality. Even given the manifest failures of such a set of rules, there are many who will nonetheless insist on clinging to them, rationalizing in one way or another that they are right and the rest of the world is wrong. A set of rules of this type is called an ideology.

ROOTS OF IDEOLOGY

All opinions are generated from emotions; an ideology is an obsession with an opinion or set of opinions, an insistence on them, an axiomatic confidence in them. But not all strongly-held opinions are ideological. If a person says that crystal healing definitely doesn't work, that's not necessarily an ideological stance. But if some form of crystal healing is invented that does work, and if it's very clearly proven to work, and the person still refuses, saying "No, crystal healing is nonsense, and any doctor who endorses it is a hack," that would be an ideological insistence. This is one sign that an idea is not just strongly held, but ideologically held: the person holding it is more interested in keeping their belief the same than considering the question of whether it is true or false.

Bear in mind, the above example is a fairly straightforward scenario; it's more difficult to draw the ideology-defining line when it comes to social theory, with which a lot of ideological beliefs are concerned. When people are interested in making judgments concerning nations, races, cultures, and other large groups of people considered collectively, a huge number of complicating factors throw a huge number of wrenches into the issue. Even merely framing such problems, selecting the right "level" on which to analyze them, can be frustratingly difficult. It's extremely easy to ignore all of these problems and make sweeping large-scale claims anyway, just by resorting to generalizations and prejudices; but it's extremely hard to take these the many complicated issues into account and make an accurate judgment. Often, the truth can't even be summed up in one single statement in the first place, and an accurate account has to be a collection of interrelated statements, each loaded with many caveats and nuances and special cases – which some people, those who prefer thinking in simple terms, aren't interested in hearing. This is why ideological beliefs concerning social matters can sometimes be hard to identify – both in others' opinions and in your own. In any case, as a general rule of thumb, a person should be willing to question their opinions and change them if one of their central assumptions should happen to be proven either incorrect, incomplete, or irrelevant. A person should not cling so hard to their beliefs that they reject the reality directly in front of them.

A common symptom of ideological obsession is a person's unwillingness to hold an intelligent conversation in which their opinions are questioned and examined. If a serious, critical conversation rapidly degenerates into a belligerent argument, wherein the objective seems to no longer be to arrive at an understanding, but rather to see who can recite rhetoric the fastest and trap the opponent in a "gotcha" moment, ideological obsession is likely afoot on one or both sides. A tendency to divert the conversation away from a slow and methodical intellectual inquiry and towards a hurried confrontation suggests a fear of properly questioning one's own beliefs. If a belief cannot stand up to a carefully constructed argument by an opponent, it's not actually very reliable, is it? Those who are heavily invested in ideology will skip past this rather obvious thought, they will allow it to vanish from their minds, if it should ever occur to them.

Obsession and ideology are derived ultimately from simple emotional inclinations. Rationalized, not rational. These deep-seated beliefs may be derived from a universal experience such as nostalgia or aesthetic pleasure, or from a small number of "imprinting" experiences, maybe even a single one. It could be either a reactionary (negative) experience, or an idealizing (positive) experience. A person gets food poisoning from a fast-food restaurant once and carries a deep vendetta against that brand for the rest of his life. A person has an early sexual experience and becomes obsessed with replicating it. The same phenomenon, a rationalization of attitudes derived from emotional experiences, is responsible for a huge number of the opinions people form, popular and unpopular, up to and including large-scale social, political, and religious issues.

Ideological views are derived from emotional sources – but it would be ridiculous to suggest that this origin makes any view invalid automatically. All opinions are derived from emotional sources in the end. This fact is highlighted to convey, to those who may be harboring ideological opinions without realizing it, that opinions cannot be assumed to be infallible; flexibility must be allowed, because an opinion derived from a limited number of experiences is itself limited, and it cannot be assumed to be some kind of absolute truth. A person's opinions should have some nuance to them, exceptions to rules, special cases that need to be specially considered, plus inadequacies in one's own experience (and thus, in one's knowledge) acknowledged. A person should be able to admit other ideas, potentially leading to change. When critically evaluating your views (a healthy mental exercise which everyone should do from time to time), you should be able to do two things. First, step back and think carefully about what concrete, corporeal facts the view is actually, centrally about, and whether, at the end of the day, it actually matters. It's very easy to form strong emotionally-motivated opinions about things that aren't actually important. If, for instance, you have a strong moral opinion about something which appears as extremely repulsive to you, maybe the thing that is so aesthetically unattractive is just that: *aesthetically* unattractive. It might not actually be as *morally* repugnant as your instincts and emotions might tempt you to believe. Second, do some research and make sure you're not missing out on any important information concerning the topic. Perhaps you will find that your repulsion to A is outweighed by an even stronger repulsion to B, something antithetical to A, such that A is the clearly preferable option (unpleasant though it may be). Or perhaps a certain thing which seems to be exceptionally repulsive is only so repulsive in rare cases with a particular common element, and it is only this common element which ought to be considered immoral, or detrimental, or what have you. And these are only two examples; there many other possible ways in which further information could reveal an opinion to be unsatisfactory. In doing this research, it's important to acknowledge any opinions that you hate, that you find truly repulsive; listen carefully to the people who espouse these opinions, and make sure you understand the actual arguments they use. Avoid the temptation to stop listening out of "disinterest," and instead try to really comprehend why they feel that way, and see whether there is something at least *resembling* a good reason behind their arguments. This is what it means to really think about both sides of an issue.

Attraction to ideology could be characterized as a response to the fear of having to answer difficult questions, to confront complex issues where a solution is not simple, to address the uncertain and unknown elements of life. Some questions simply do not have an answer that can be looked up in some authoritative textbook. Maybe there is not a single, unambiguous answer, but rather, many different answers for different circumstances. Maybe there is a single answer, but it requires a long and difficult explanation that in turn requires specialized knowledge to comprehend. Maybe the question itself is so elusive that even grasping the true meaning of the thing being asked about is a significant part of the challenge. Or perhaps the question is actually not meaningful at all, and its seeming importance is only the result of some popular person or historically-respected organization trying to make it seem so. To the person who wishes for the world to be simple and easily comprehensible, and who hates to admit that they are wrong, these are all threatening notions; ideology provides the easy way out, an excuse to not think too hard, an "absolute truth" that can be referenced infallibly. Contrast this attitude with that of the cold person mentioned in Part II, who is simply disinterested in answering such questions. The ideologue is the person who, faced with a difficult question, wishes to be able to answer that question quickly, easily, and decisively – but without having to do much work to arrive at that answer. The cold person, on the other hand, dismisses the question with a conclusive "I don't care."

PIGEONHOLING AND TEMPTATION

There is a tempting thought, watching the perpetual battle of thousands of conflicting ideologies in any given realm of discourse, that one of them is simply correct and all of the others are simply wrong. But this is an illusion, a fantasy, an easy way out of forging one's own identity, one's own opinions. It is the excuse made by a lazy mind to pigeonhole one's identity, attaching oneself to some kind of pre-existing dogma or other ideology, in order to have the critical elements of one's identity determined in advance. Any attempt at selecting entire swathes of one's identity from a set of pre-made options, as casually as one might select a dish from a menu, is destined to lead to disappointment. The moment a hole appears in the ideology, a question which it cannot answer, or an insistence that it makes which one cannot agree with, or even more obviously, an internal contradiction, the entire structure comes into question. If the immersion breaks, if the idea that the ideology is perfect and irrefutable is no more, the ideology ceases to serve its purpose as a ready-made catch-all solution. And what comes next, after the abandonment of one ideology? Is it as simple as switching to a different one? Many people will do this when one ideology fails, and many people will continue to be surprised and disappointed that the new one also fails a few years later, if not sooner. Each new ideology will have its own holes, its own insufficiencies. The temptation to tie oneself to such-and-such religious dogma, such-and-such political ideology, or any other similar thing will never lead to satisfaction. How about simply having your own opinions? Is that such an unreasonable option? Or is it absolutely necessary to pigeonhole yourself, to fit into some pre-existing group, even at the cost of putting your real beliefs to the side? To some people, yes, it actually *does* seem unreasonable; to them, the notion of having *no* attachment to any ideology-associated group whatsoever is a radical one, as frightening as the prospect of suddenly disappearing from society and living in a shack in the woods somewhere, off the grid. The social temptation to be "part of a group" is enormous.

The people who will be most susceptible to ideological possession will be those who do not know what their real beliefs are, or rather, those who do not yet have real beliefs. If a person is indoctrinated into some ideology or other from childhood, they will often deliberately rebel against it once they get older. Perhaps they will later decide to accept some fraction of the ideology after all, or perhaps they will abandon it entirely; either way, it is only after they have experience with both the ideology and something contrary to it that they can form a more genuine opinion, a more real belief. But there are some people who grow up and never perform this kind of critical thinking exercise, who continue to insist upon one ideology, having swallowed every bit of its doctrine (either what they grew up with or something else discovered later in life, after their original ideology proved inadequate). Despite being firmly tied to one particular direction in life, these people are, at heart, directionless; their only sense of direction is dictated by a force that they simply decided to cling to one day and never stopped. If the speaker for an ideological group that this person is tied to suddenly changes their position, or implicitly reveals that they told a lie in the past, the follower will not care, and will allow themselves to be dragged along. And if they are somehow jerked away from their ideology of choice, these directionless individuals will instantaneously jump to and cling to some other ideology, having abruptly decided that it is the solution to all questions of morality or public policy or whatever else. It goes without saying that a decision of that magnitude is not one that should be made in such a hurry.

The temptation to seek out an ideology, perhaps an extreme ideology, might also be driven by a traumatic experience. The power of such experiences on the mind should not be underestimated, especially on the young and impressionable. Perhaps one is involved in a violent confrontation, or hears about an exceptionally atrocious event occurring somewhere far away. Even a single instance of being accosted by an especially obnoxious, mean person might be enough to dramatically impact a person's opinion of whatever group the perpetrator belongs to (or seems to belong to).

After experiencing an event like that, with negative emotions weighing heavily on the mind, it may be tempting to "do research" on such-and-such group to learn more about them. Maybe the group is affiliated with a certain political opinion, or a certain race or nationality, or a certain religion. Doing serious research is one thing, but it's quite another to solely do the sort of "research" that just so happens to consistently make the group in question look bad. If the temptation to seek out this kind of thing should occur to you, be very careful to weigh your priorities: avoid seeking out things for the sole purpose of making yourself angry, and avoid finding too much pleasure in hating other people – even if you think they deserve to be hated – even if they *actually do* deserve to be hated. This is a very popular pastime, baffling though it might sound when it is explained for what it really is. Proof of its popularity can be easily found: there are an infinite number of resources available, especially in the age of the Internet, to allow a person to find material that makes *any* group look bad, and that makes a person of *any* opinion angry. If a person wants to be angry at such-and-such group, material that supports this emotional response is available at a moment's notice, no matter what the group. This strange pastime is tempting because it produces an impression that agrees with that given by the initial traumatic encounter: it is a reinforcement of one's own existing impressions and opinions. It is obvious that forming a habit out of this kind of "researching" is dangerous; it is a direct route to cementing one's own rashly-developed opinions with a constant stimulus of confirmation bias. It would not be difficult to develop an extreme opinion in this way, and a person with a deeply-ingrained opinion of that sort may easily find themselves one day publicly doing or saying something completely stupid and embarrassing – or worse, instigating violence.

This is one example of why careful and skeptical inspection of one's own opinions is necessary. How many people hold extreme opinions that are ultimately only derived from a single misfortune? How many people hold poor opinions of certain groups because they had the displeasure of witnessing the very worst and most extreme of those groups? Imagine, for example, that a person is very strongly tied to one far end of the political spectrum because they wish to separate themselves from the obnoxious, arrogant, hypocritical, violent members of the opposite side. Imagine that they point to dozens, even hundreds, of examples which they can pull up from online videos and news articles, saying, "Do you see these people? How can *they* be in the right?" But in reality, these are the worst examples. These reports of strange people and unusual events which are the most conducive to being spread, these occurrences which are the most shocking and outrageous, are spread so efficiently *because* they are extreme and unusual. Not everyone on the opposite side of the political spectrum holds the absolute most extreme version of that opposite set of opinions. No one whose opinions are worth their salt will actually defend the kind of intolerant, vitriolic behavior that tends to make news headlines and trending videos. And it should not be surprising whatsoever that those who hold the most deranged and dogmatic opinions are also some of the most vocal. When seeking out material to become angry at, the extremists will be the first ones to appear in the spotlight. Therefore, one should be careful to avoid jumping from the instinctive reaction "this person is doing something bad" to the more ideological "everyone who holds a similar opinion to this person's is bad." In much the same way that violent revenge only perpetuates a cycle of violence, taking a reactionary stance against someone else's ideology only breeds more reactionary ideology – in both directions.

RATIONAL

To preface the upcoming discussion of ideology, there are certain aspects of the rational mind that ought to be examined. There are many people who look at their own behavior, wonder why they do what they do, and say to themselves, "I don't know." To give a reason why is to have the rational mind make a judgment about the utility or preferability of such-and-such action – it might be nice if human beings were rational animals, if everything that we do was done for a rational reason; but we are not, even if some people are still deluded enough to think that we are.

The reason why this is not the case is shown by the Munchhausen Trilemma. If every action a person takes has a reason behind it, a justification, then the arrival at that justification must have another reason behind it, a second justification. And the arrival at the second justification must have a third justification behind it, and so on. Where is the end of this? Or is there even an end at all? The Trilemma states that there are only three possibilities: either the sequence extends to an infinite regress, wraps around itself in a circular line of reasoning, or stops by reaching a "final justification" that is held to be true axiomatically and is considered to require no further justification. It is this third option, the axiomatic option, which is actually used by the human brain. It is widely understood that the brain does certain things automatically, but it is not so widely understood that such automatic things, such as involuntary instinctive and emotional reactions, are the roots of all human reasoning and all human "rational" thought. But in order to avoid the nonsensical "What the Tortoise Said to Achilles"-esque concept of a finite brain undergoing an infinite regress of reasons and rationalizations upon every single decision, or the logical nonsense of a circular proof, this is the only conclusion possible.

In ordinary tasks of reasoning, a person may consider his reasoning process to consist of analyzing a situation, determining whether such-and-such action is rational or not, and acting accordingly. But this "reasoning process" in-the-moment is only a tiny fragment of the actual process which resulted in this particular judgment. The mind is not a calculator which makes such decisions instantaneously; the information necessary to make that decision was not always there. When this person was a small child (let alone an infant), he did not undergo this same predictive process. The rational part of the mind has the ability to predict whether an activity is rational *before* doing it, but this predictive power can only be exercised after days and months and years of experience carrying out the other task: the task of *rationalizing* actions that were performed *without thinking,* after the fact, based on their consequences. The automatic processes of the brain, the instinctual and emotional responses which are performed without rational thought, these are what lie at the bottom of rational thought; these are the "axioms" of the rational mind. Note that the word "axiom" is used here not because these inclinations represent an actual unquestionable truth, but because they come *first*, that they are the responses which occur in the mind (or, more generally, the body) *without* prior consideration and justification.

A child performs actions without thinking. The rational part of the mind analyzes the consequences – if they are desirable consequences, the rational mind comes to believe that the action was rational, appropriate, justified. With years of experience, the mind will learn to categorize sets of rational actions by determining the common factors in their success, the reasons that they succeeded – and this information will later be used to predict whether similar actions will have desirable consequences ahead of time. In parallel, if an action has undesirable consequences, the mind will feel guilt, and will come to believe that the action was irrational, inappropriate, unjustified. The mind will, again, categorize sets of irrational actions by determining the reasons why they failed, and this will, again, be used for predictive purposes later.

The fact that children – all children – perform actions without thinking was illustrated in Bill Cosby's popular stand-up segment concerning "brain damage." A child does something they "know" they are not supposed to do, someone asks them why they did it, and the child says, despairing, "I don't know." The image speaks for itself. Of course, adults also act without thinking, some more than others; and those who act without thinking too frequently (and especially in sensitive contexts) are considered to be stupid or irresponsible or unconscientious, even if they have the ability to come up with rationalizations – they are considered stupid because their rationalizations don't "make sense," because (according to the standards and rationalizations of most individuals) their rationalizations are actually irrational. When a conscientious person does something which they don't have a rationalization for, or worse, which is contrary to their previously established notions of rationality, they feel guilty about it, and they ask themselves, despairing, "Why did I do this thing? Is something wrong with me? That was so stupid of me." Those who are still immature enough to want to consider themselves "totally rational," those who cannot bear the thought of acting foolishly out of emotion or instinct, will feel this sensation especially strongly, perhaps too strongly for their own good. Unfortunately for their egos, a sizeable portion of everything that they do comes from emotion or instinct – they're just good at rationalizing it under most circumstances.

The consequence of the above is that many people have a desire to wrap up every aspect of their life into a box of rationality, into a neat and organized set of rules that work for every situation. From this desire emerge ideology and dogma – methods of "rational" decision-making which are ostensibly all-encompassing, but which in reality are too simple (one might even say, too stupid) to achieve this lofty goal. In reality, it is a far more nuanced set of rules that will be required in order to be comprehensive, so nuanced in fact that these rules will have to vary from person to person in accordance with the peculiarities of each individual's life. Trying to create a comprehensive set of rules that work for everyone simply will not succeed; this is why, in democratic nations, the law only coerces behavior that almost everyone agrees warrants coercing – the things that almost everyone's diverse experiences of rationalization agree to warrant coercing. These things constitute the most basic principles of tolerable behavior; more advanced goals, such as being a good person, require the development of additional personal rules that may not be applicable to everybody, or that not everybody may agree about, particularly on the details. It is therefore not within the scope of the law to mandate being a good person – only being a tolerable person.

The rationalization function of the mind is fundamental and powerful, and it is responsible for some of the behaviors described in Part II, such as the sustainment of an equilibrium of inaction. It is also responsible for the rationalization of ideological beliefs, of course; these beliefs and obsessions have their deepest roots in simple emotional responses, and so, on an emotional level, it is very tempting to simply cling to an ideology once it is formed, and to consider oneself correct in doing so. Therefore, many people will (if only subconsciously) rationalize their emotionally-driven ideological ideas, saying to themselves that they are rational, logical, objectively correct. Combined with the socially-driven desire to be a part of a group, one can then go further, and rationalize pigeonholing oneself, pinning oneself to an existing ideological structure associated with a group or type of person. The following sections will discuss the common emotional phenomena that result in the opinions which eventually form ideologies, and the processes by which ideologies are rationalized. Some readers may be neck-deep in ideological thought and not even recognize it – hopefully, the descriptions that follow will serve as helpful warning signs.

PROJECTION AND PROPAGANDA

An important factor in the development of ideological beliefs is the projection of personal tastes onto opinions about the world at large. A person's preferences, their ideas about how they want to live their individual life, may become transformed into judgments of right and wrong, and perhaps even judgments of what should be legal and illegal.

For example, picture a stereotypical anti-gay conservative type. This person might justify their opinion in several ways, perhaps dogmatically ("This sacred text says that homosexual activity is bad") or perhaps naturalistically ("Homosexual activity is contrary to the natural way of things") or perhaps by digging up some statistics or a collection of individual incidents that somehow make homosexuals look bad. This person would describe one or all of these as "evidence" for their beliefs; but what if this is only a rationalization? Which is more likely: that a person observed this evidence and *then* developed their anti-gay attitude, or that the anti-gay attitude was *already present in the individual*, and only later rationalized? The latter is more likely, because it is significantly easier for a person to adopt an opinion which rationalizes their own taste than to develop an entirely new opinion, especially an unpopular opinion. If a person is strictly heterosexual, one could say that they have a "distaste" for the image of homosexual activity; they, personally, do not want to look at such imagery, it is not attractive to them. For some people, this aspect of their sexual preference, this "distaste," could then be projected beyond the realm of individual taste, into a "disagreement" or "dislike" of homosexual activity or imagery at large. The sentiment would change from "I don't want to do this" to "people shouldn't do this." An even more extreme projection would be to the realm of "nobody should be allowed to do this," that is, a desire to see laws enacted which would prohibit homosexual activities, or even criminalize expressions of the sexual preference. "I don't like this thing, therefore, it should be illegal." Of course, the type of person to hold such an opinion as this will never rationalize it in so few words, and certainly not to themselves. They will have plenty of rhetoric and "evidence" which they will cite as the true reasons.

When it comes to the role of "evidence" in the development of an ideological belief in the above sense, the first word that comes to mind is "propaganda." Using the same example, is it possible for an indifferent person, someone with no real opinion on the matter, to see a piece of anti-gay propaganda and to have their mind swayed? Yes and no. A person could be swayed by such a thing, but in order for this to occur, they would need to already have both the "distaste" for homosexuality and the kind of judgmental or intolerant personality that would make them susceptible to such propaganda. In other words, they would need the kind of personality traits that would make them likely to develop an anti-gay attitude in any case; so calling them an "indifferent" person wouldn't have been accurate in the first place. A truly indifferent person would probably lean by default toward the popular opinion, which is that homosexuality is fine, or at least tolerable, and would disapprove of the propaganda's message.

Some would be more pessimistic, suggesting that certain forms of propaganda are so dangerous that they should not be permitted at all, that they should be excluded from the protection of free speech. But this raises a difficult philosophical question: to what degree should we assume that people are capable of critical thinking? To say that propaganda is dangerous is to say that people can be predictably affected by it in a negative way. How predictably? Are people merely a medium by which propaganda and advertising can be reliably translated into votes and sales? Some people do seem to move predictably, always following trends and ads, but others seem to be more independently-minded, more willing to think for themselves; but the real issue seems to be the fact that a large body of people will always have a lowest common denominator, that there will always exist some method of propaganda which can affect a *mass* of people predictably, should it be broadcast broadly enough. How should the law, which is applied to the population as a whole, respond to this situation? This is a very difficult question whose answer falls outside the scope of this book, but which the reader is encouraged to think about.

Returning to the notion of projection, let's consider the more general case. If a person is going to vote for some kind of policy change, which is more likely? That they will vote for what they personally find most attractive, or what they think is "best for society"? How many people even differentiate between these things? To be specific, how many people have an intense personal *dislike* for a certain activity, which they would vote *in favor of* (even to the point of voting to decriminalize it if it is illegal, or voting against criminalizing it if it is legal), for the sake of a higher ideal? How many people have the integrity to honestly say "I don't like what you're doing, but I'll defend to the death your right to do it"? It's a noble and magnanimous thing to say – if you said this, would it be the truth?

The projection phenomenon is a form of rationalization – the rationalization of some kind of directed (e.g., restrictive) belief based on one's own emotional responses, one's personal taste, one's ideas on how one would like to direct (e.g., restrict) one's own life. It is the rationalization that says "I feel good about this, therefore, this must be truly good" – or "I feel bad about this, therefore, this must be truly bad." It is something that a person will need to learn to recognize and let go of in order to overcome dependence on ideology, to escape the habit of thinking in simple terms, and in general to develop a more nuanced view of the world. One should be particularly careful of any strong opinions that are motivated by a sense of anger, fear, or disgust; they could well fall into this category.

IDEOLOGY AS AESTHETIC

When it comes to the initial adoption of an ideology, the most tempting features are those that a given individual can associate with their own life, even if only in a superficial way. One way to do this is by simply adopting the ideology of those around them – this is how children can be "brainwashed" by their parents or other adults into believing strange things – and another way is by selecting an ideology with an aesthetic that the individual finds appealing. If the person is in a position where they believe they "have to" have an ideology to follow (if not the even worse case, that the ideology of those around them is the absolute truth, and that they "have to" follow it in order to be correct), then they will often select whatever seems most appealing at first glance, and rationalize their selection of it later. This is essentially an ideological instance of post-purchase rationalization.

Various ideologies have various aesthetics, and different people like different aesthetics, in accordance with their personal tastes; while it is possible (even desirable) to have a person's aesthetic preferences be totally independent of their beliefs and practices, it is often the case that the "projecting" behavior described in the last section will emerge: the person's aesthetic tastes will bleed into their ideas about how the world ought to work.

There is the aesthetic of purity, and of the corruption of purity. There is the aesthetic of order, and of chaos. There is the aesthetic of respecting tradition, and of rebelling against tradition. There is the aesthetic of the person born into greatness, and of the person who worked from nothing to achieve greatness. There is the aesthetic of hierarchy, and of equality. There is the aesthetic of competition, and of cooperation. There is the aesthetic of law, and of revolution. There is the aesthetic of conquest, and of peace. All of these things are aesthetic tastes that may be held totally independently of one's theories about culture and policy.

The interest in the aesthetic qualities of an ideology may only be an initial attracting factor, or it may persist and remain one of a person's main reasons for associating with that ideology. In the cases where a person is more interested in the aesthetic of an ideology than the ideology's actual theories and affiliated practices, strange behaviors can be observed. For example, it may happen that a person will seem to be wholly devoted to the ideology, but will be unable to provide basic information about it; or worse, that they will become irate at the mere imposition of ordinary, obvious, even politely-asked questions. This is an indicator that this person has not really thought about the ideology itself very carefully, and only enjoys the aesthetic of it, and perhaps the sensation of discussing relevant ideas with their peer group – everyone being in near-total agreement with each other on every issue, of course. This phenomenon affects both popular ideologies and fringe ideologies. Obsession with an ideology that one is only interested in for superficial reasons, and which one has not carefully investigated and critically evaluated, can lead to troublesome situations. The least of these would be blurting out something stupid in a public setting, believing it to be totally and unquestionably true because it matches the aesthetic of the ideology. There have been cases of CEOs and other high-ranking persons being made to resign over scandals of exactly this type. Some people subconsciously fear this kind of scenario, and hide their ideological beliefs, declining to comment on political or social issues; this suggests that the person's interest in the ideology is more superficial than they are willing to admit to themselves. If you happen to find yourself doing this, a good response is to look for the contradiction or dubious element in your beliefs or actions, isolate the issue, and try to rectify it; a bad response is to deliberately ignore it, double down on the ideological attachment, and perpetuate the state of cognitive dissonance.

It is important here to note that a person might come to *think* that they are interested in certain ideas or events, but not actually be interested. A person might *feel* like they're obligated to take an interest in something, and they might attach themselves to certain ideas, *trying* to care, but ultimately not care enough to analyze the situation on a deeper level. This is one circumstance that can lead to people develop very strong opinions based on aesthetic qualities alone, and then finding themselves woefully unprepared when asked for an explanation of *their own beliefs*.

The other main pitfalls of swallowing an ideology for aesthetic reasons are obvious. A person obsessed with the aesthetic of purity may, for example, come to think that sex and reproduction should be policed, in order to make the population itself "pure." Someone who becomes obsessed with the aesthetic of anarchy may start wantonly burning down buildings at random. Someone who becomes obsessed with the aesthetic of sexual liberty might decide that they have the sovereign right to rape whomever they want. And so on. Of course, just because a person is not in such an extreme ideological category as this does not mean that they have completely avoided the pitfalls of ideology as aesthetic – there are many lesser offenses than these that are still offenses. Someone who is too insistent upon an ideology, who considers it to be some kind of supreme moral imperative, might abandon their friends or be themselves abandoned due to their constant and annoying insistence. Someone could donate large quantities of their hard-earned money to a charitable cause, ostensibly associated with an attractive ideological aesthetic, unaware that the lion's share of this money will wind up in some charlatan's pockets, under the label of "administrative fees."

Many non-ideological examples of preoccupation with aesthetics can be seen in everyday life. A film is permitted by the review board to portray considerable violence, including murder, and get away with a PG-13 rating – but having more than one or two instances of the word "fuck" is not permitted, otherwise it has to be rated R. This joke of a rating guideline remains common practice in the American film industry to this day. It is not that the fact of profanity is considered worse than the fact of murder, but rather, the aesthetic of profanity is considered more offensive than the aesthetic of murder. Compare this with the amusing trend of military organizations and their contractors (in some countries) being very overt in their public advertisements about how non-discriminatory they are, in terms of equal employment opportunity, inclusion, and such. If their target audience thinks employment discrimination is bad, wait until they learn about what goes on in war. Yes, it is very possible for bizarre results to emerge in public relations campaigns where aesthetics are considered more important than substance.

Another such case can be seen in corporations who are happy to extol the virtues of liberty and equality while quietly (or, perhaps, not so quietly) using sweatshops in third-world countries to mass-manufacture their products for the cheapest possible price. Why does such a thing occur? Because the customers of such a company are, if their purchasing patterns are any indicator, *not interested* in whether slave labor was employed to make the product in question; aside from their primary interest, the product itself, they are only interested in how friendly of a message the corporation seems to convey, if that. Most consumers will never even think about asking the most commonplace ethical questions: for instance, whether child laborers and/or slaves were involved in their production. Not to mention the more complex questions, such as whether the nation in which the goods are being produced is some kind of banana republic, or a client state under a totalitarian regime. Ask yourself: when was the last time you bought any mass-manufactured article, such as a shirt or a phone, and even *considered* the question of whether slavery or child labor were involved, before confirming your decision to make the purchase?

As long as the corporation's marketing scheme has the aesthetic of liberty (and again, even this is optional), the non-liberated status of their production environment is irrelevant for the average consumer. And here's the punch line: even if a whistleblower or human rights organization exposes a company for such atrocities, often the public will not care, because the fact of the injustice is so distant from them. Indeed, they will only care, if at all, for the few fleeting moments that the event is still making headlines in the news. Contrast this with how rapidly the public will arrange protests and boycotts if a high-level representative of a company makes some kind of public gaffe, the very embarrassing kind that gets a lot of publicity, something that doesn't really hurt anybody, but which violates that *aesthetic* of humanitarianism – and not only how inflamed the public will be about it, but for how long of a period will they remain vindictive afterwards! Appalling though it might be to know that such trivial events are what capture the attention of the public, consider the incredible effort that would be required to make every person in a population into an educated consumer. Consider how many people do not care about such things, who do not *want* to care, whose opinions about a company or government agency would not change even given evidence, or better yet, *admission by the organization themselves,* of massive human rights violations. The only things that can change the mind of such an indifferent populace are the lowest common denominators of emotional appeal, one of which is aesthetics.

The importance of aesthetics to almost any organization can be seen in the common methods of developing a brand image. It's essentially been proven by this point in history, to the degree of being common knowledge, that superficial aesthetic elements sell. Sex sells, obviously, and attractive people in general sell, even if the product or service being sold has no relevance whatsoever to physical appearance. This is true not only in the commercial realm, but in the ideological realm as well. Consider the archetypal political cartoon, the omnipresent formula of "attractive person right, ugly person wrong." Morally right and morally wrong, that is – ostensibly characteristics which are totally orthogonal to physical appearance. While a person's activities (the manifestations of their beliefs) may contribute to some degree to their appearance, a serious argument for a causal relationship between the one and the other is seldom the point of such a cartoon. The point is something much more immediate: to elicit in the reader positive emotions associated with one opinion, and negative emotions with the opposite opinion. If the proliferation of this trope means anything, it is that one of the most consistently effective emotional motivators of political thought is the superficial, the aesthetic.

NO INFORMATION

It's not very difficult to deduce why aesthetics have such impressive power over the general population: people react emotionally to aesthetics, and emotional reactions are the basis on which all other "rational" beliefs are formed, that is, rationalized. The emotional reaction is quick and easy to induce in people, if you have the means to convey a message to a large audience – it does not require the audience to go to the trouble of doing research or cross-checking various sources of information, nothing at all like that. All that is needed, for the fastest results in influencing large numbers of people, is to give them an aesthetic signal that they will immediately respond to emotionally. Just think about it: will the average person catch themselves in the middle of an emotional response, and try to deliberately separate their aesthetic values from their opinions on how the world should be? Of course not. Only very rarely will a person show that much restraint. It is far easier, and thus far more common, for a person to assume by default that they are correct, and thus, that their emotional response is something that they should incorporate (rationalize) into their worldview. It is not until this kind of emotional response is met with a negative consequence that this rationalization will be inhibited – and if a person is in the comfort of their home, merely reading a news headline or a social media post, they are very distant from negative consequences. Indeed, negative consequences will not appear until this person's hastily-developed opinions start bleeding into their actions, and they bring trouble upon themselves one way or another. Unfortunately, by the time this occurs, the individual will sometimes be too deeply entrenched in their ideology to be willing to admit that a particular negative consequence is cause for serious ideological reconsideration. Such a person, if their actions have led to their embarrassment in public, could easily tell themselves that they are being persecuted for speaking the truth.

In other words, it's common for a person to form opinions, and even quite strong opinions, based on next to no information besides the aesthetic. A person's "research" into relevant issues will often be doused in confirmation bias, that is, the inclination towards seeking out opinions which agree with one's own, and avoiding the opposite. This creates the situation where, if a person has decided (or fooled themselves into believing) that such-and-such thing is of critical importance to them, their method of making a judgment about this thing will often be based on no more than the superficial, the aesthetic. The indifferent voter who admits to preferring whichever candidate "speaks better" is more honest than the dedicated news-watcher who insists that one candidate is utterly superior to the other based on scarcely any additional information. Campaign promises convey no information and no obligations. Most of the details of a candidate's past activity while in office are utterly unknowable to any person not "on the inside," so to speak. Even if some of the consequences of their actions are observable to the public, the motivations behind them (which might be considerably more justified or less justified than they appear) can't be meaningfully evaluated without access to contextual facts which are necessarily kept under the tightest confidentiality. And of course, the apparent consequences of their activities are only a fraction of the total consequences. It is only a very tiny amount of pertinent information that makes it to the dedicated "informed" voter, much less the average voter. Before the votes are cast, nothing is certain: any element of a political campaign could be a mere act, a publicity stunt. "Politics is the entertainment division of the military-industrial complex." However, this very tiny amount of pertinent information is not truly zero information. Even in such difficult and obscure fields as politics, it is possible to acquire useful knowledge – if only a limited amount. Concrete facts *can* be determined here and there, but as for an in-depth understanding of the overall picture, and a reliable estimate of how a candidate would actually perform once elected? I wouldn't hold my breath.

Organizations, and those who represent them, have an incentive to create an image for themselves, a collection of superficial elements to present to the public. This is the brand image: an image to be held in the mind of the public, as to what the organization is "about," what values they represent. As explained, this can be entirely irrelevant to their cause and only present in their public relations affairs due to the importance of aesthetics to the public. Similarly, moving back down to the individual case, each person will have certain elements of their character that they present to others – and certain elements that they do not. The individual's selectiveness in this matter results in a self-characterization, something similar to a brand image, but with more flexibility; a person can choose how much they want to reveal about themselves depending on who they're talking to. In general, some people are more candid, and some people are more secretive, depending on personality and circumstances. But in any case, it is important for a person not to let their presentation of themselves become an actual façade, an actual lie. The person who does this will not only have to deal with the stress of constantly putting up an act contrary to their real nature, but also of *knowing* that they are lying (if they are conscientious), or else the practical consequences of either *not knowing* or *not caring* if they are lying (if they are in denial, delusional, or otherwise in a strange state of mind). While there may be elements of your character that you choose not to share with certain people at certain times, you don't want your self-characterization to become warped out of proportion – communication is difficult enough without adding complications like this. Finally, it's important to note that the image that you present to others can affect your own self-image, your perception of yourself. This is sometimes useful; when someone (a young person especially) doesn't really know what they want, they may experiment and do things spontaneously, and see what gets a good reception from the people around them, attaching themselves to the ideas and behaviors that "work." This is fine; it's a natural part of the learning process. But at some point, the person will start to recognize that there are certain things that they genuinely like, regardless of the opinions of the people around them. A person in this position should beware of two kinds of self-censorship: Lying to people about what they really like, and even worse, lying to *themselves,* saying that because others don't like this thing, they themselves must not like it either.

PREJUDICE

One of the most common and pervasive forms of ideology is prejudice, the passing of heavy judgment on a person based on a small amount of information, especially superficial physical qualities such as skin color. This inclination is common due to the primordial and powerful instinct of "my group good, other group bad" which is present to some degree in everyone, a vestige of the early tribal years of the human species. This phenomenon is also not limited to race or sex, or even to groups identifiable by physical traits - any method of conceptualizing people as being categorized into groups can pave the way for the same thing.

But how does the ideological stance itself form? Even if the instinct described above is universal, particular prejudices are not. Something more is required. One such factor could be plain fear of the unknown; a person encounters a type of person that they have never seen before, and which they know next to nothing about. Some people will be inclined to immediately consider the stranger to be a threat, and will either run away or try to fight the person off. This type of response can even occur outside of physical interactions; a person reads about an unknown or "different" sort of person in print or on the Internet and has the same emotional reaction, either trying to distract themselves from thinking about it or vocalizing their distaste for this new and unusual character. A person who exhibits this behavior frequently can be considered to have an obsession; a person who additionally goes to the trouble of rationalizing why their characteristic manner of response is correct is an ideologue.

Another motivator toward a prejudiced ideology could be a small number of traumatic experiences. Imagine a person who has had, in their entire life, only one memorable experience interacting with, say, a black person, and that this experience was an unpleasant one. A single traumatic experience can very powerfully affect a person's opinion – a person in this position could be inclined towards racism, and it would take deliberate effort on this person's part to turn themselves away from their emotional response and think about things more critically. Even if this inclination is the product of *all of the information they have* – it's still only a small amount of information. Naturally, it would help, by way of accumulating more information, for this person to have a larger number of opportunities to interact with people of other races in friendly circumstances. Similarly, the phenomenon of this trauma-association is likely to naturally decrease as the person gets older and has more life experience; younger people, then, are more susceptible to this kind of association. There are many opportunities in life for a person to step back and think about being more tolerant; but what if this person simply doesn't bother? What if this person *insists* that their initially-formed opinion is correct, and what if they prefer to rationalize it, and do confirmation-biased "research" to try and justify it, and end up restricting their worldview all the more heavily instead? This is one way that ideological obsession can appear. Luckily, this particular form is becoming more and more unfashionable as it becomes more and more obvious that it's impractical to make such hasty generalizations about individuals based on broad group membership alone. Unfashionable in polite society, that is – a lot of society has yet to become polite.

RESTRICTION AND TOTALITARIANISM

Some ideologues preach that the path to a virtuous life can only be achieved through coercion – that a powerful force must impose the people to work hard in order to sustain themselves, or else the people will suffer from boredom and unfulfilling lives, or turn to vice and become self-destructive and destructive of others. But this is wrong – it is only a psychological projection of the person who loves to work for others, who loves to be given orders, or else the person who fantasizes about being the one to give orders.

Those who would argue that restricting one's life is a necessity for freedom (that is, in the sense that people should be given rigid orders in many aspects of their lives) will typically bring forth arguments that hinge on a linguistic trick: the claim that "restrictions" or "limitations" are necessary conditions for a healthy or successful life is practically a tautology. A human life, being finite, is naturally limited; deliberate actions occur at the opportunity cost of other actions, and so those other actions must be "restricted" in order to execute the desired action; people who live successful lives are generally organized, which implies that they "limit" the amount and types of recreation in their lives; et cetera. These things are so obvious that they are truisms, but they can be rephrased through rhetoric that suggests that restricting one's life is something inherently good, that rigidity and conformity are, on general principle, superior to flexibility and creativity. Even though this proposition is on such a high level of abstraction that judgments based on it can't be anything other than situational, it still occurs in ideological rhetoric.

To play devil's advocate, what does it mean to never place restrictions on one's own life? Consider the fake hedonist described in Part II, the person who has no desires whatsoever except to be entertained, who will indulge in superficial pleasures simply "because they can," and who will refuse to adopt healthy lifestyle changes "because they don't have to." This person might say to themselves that they are living a life unrestricted, but this is not the case. Many of the fake hedonist's decisions will be extremely restrictive, even more so than the restrictions they reject as unnecessary. If someone chooses to never leave a basement because they "don't have to," is that choice liberating? Is that an exercise of freedom? If someone chooses to stare into a screen for 12 hours a day, devoid of any kind of conscious thought, is that person "free"? The unsavory image of this type of person is something that restrictive ideologues will often appeal to: the audience does not wish to become this miserable excuse for a person, so they will turn towards the opposite. But thinking a little bit harder about this character will reveal that they are also restricting their life; and the restrictions that are offered by some ideologue will not necessarily lead to a better life than that simply by virtue of being restrictions. Even the fact that they are *deliberate* restrictions is not necessarily an improvement – a person can deliberately restrict themselves in many ways without finding the way that is right for them.

There are many who do not trust themselves to behave autonomously, and who love to be controlled and ordered, because it gives their life a singular and obvious purpose. And the more powerful and demanding the commanding body, the better – if you are forced to do something at gunpoint, you have no need whatsoever to doubt either the purpose or utility of your existence. You are in fact utterly incapable of encountering difficult existential questions, because your entire mind is occupied, focused on staying alive and ensuring that your masters do not consider you a threat. These people, who love to obey, and who wish that all of society consisted of coercion, ordering and obeying, should be ignored. There are many endorsers of totalitarianism with personalities of this sort, who would absolutely love for some kind of totalitarian dictator to rise to power. Maybe such a person is very secretive about their beliefs, and would never dare show open support for a rising dictator – but who would immediately submit to the dictatorship should it actually be established, saying something like "It would be madness to go against the people in power," or the classic "I'm just following orders." There's a definite laziness in this type of character, a "banality of evil." It's an extreme sort of laziness – this person wishes for (their concept of) peace of mind so badly that they will conform to anything that the status quo seems to demand, even if it demands complicity with or direct involvement in incredible acts of cruelty.

Interestingly, more rarely, there is also an equal and opposite character: the anarcho-primitivist who wishes not to be restricted and coerced by a ruler, but instead by nature and by lack of resources. They wish to be forced into poverty and wilderness, such that they not only *can* live the idealistic simple life that they desire, but such that *they have no other option*. The critical aspect of both the desire to be forced into deprivation and the desire to be ruled over by a tyrant stem from the desire for a person to *have their decisions forced upon them so that they do not have to think*. They wish to enter a sustained environment, an equilibrium, with *no ambiguity* as to the purpose or utility or morality of their actions – a very *simple* set of requirements, a *clear and obvious* goal at any given time. In other words, they wish for life to be a simple and straightforward game instead of an open-ended and complex one. Note here the intersection of two instincts – the desire to remain in equilibrium and the desire to conceptualize the world in simple terms. This is in accordance with the "negative desires" described in Part II, those desires which have noticeable similarities to a death wish.

TO EXERT POWER

The ideological/obsessive types associated with violence and warmongering are baffling to many people. Why would anybody like war? Why do we, as a species, even bother with it when it's so horrific? It seems as though nobody actively wants it (hence the names of military organizations often including the euphemistic terms "Defense" or "Security") and yet new wars consistently keep appearing, one after the other. What is the motivation behind it?

What is the psychological state that would make a person want to lead an invasion of a country out of the blue, or to support such a thing?

The short answer is: it's fun to exert power over other people. Think of video games. Think of the most commonplace power fantasies, including revenge fantasies, the fantasy of correcting or chastising someone who's wrong, and the fantasy of rescuing a population from a villain. This is one kind of temptation towards violence and coercion. Doing things that you're not allowed to do is also fun; and initiating violence is almost always something one is "not allowed to do." The power fantasies associated with this go without saying. Consider the things which are unacceptable or forbidden, which you do in secret. Perhaps some part of your "rational" mind even believes that these things are bad and shouldn't be done, but you do them anyway, because of the attractiveness of the forbidden, of making the impossible possible, of expanding the limits of experience. Think of the mysterious force that compels you to do these things in spite of your "rational" reasoning. It is this same force which compels "bad people" to do "bad things." Sade wrote extensively on the subject, suggesting a strong association between the urge to commit violence and the sexual urge itself.

It's fun to exert power over other people; but those who never have had the chance to exert power over others, or (perhaps more commonly) those who have had such chances and who have never taken advantage of them, will often come to rationalize their actions as "correct" – they will consider themselves morally righteous for not interfering with others' lives. People who do this too often become ineffectual and timid, avoidant of other people altogether for fear of offending them. But what about the opposite case, those who give in to the compulsion, and force their power onto others? If someone does this often enough without facing negative consequences (or at least, what they *perceive* as negative consequences), then once again, this person will begin to rationalize what they have done. They will believe that not only is it acceptable, but maybe even *righteous* to try to force onto others physical violence, or ideology, or to use lies, threats, extortion, theft, or any number of other devices to exert power over their enemy or dupe. The most common format for this type of rationalization is the idea that one's beliefs are simply right, and the proof that they are right is that practicing them works. Inversely, the targeted person must simply be wrong, because they *can* be defeated or duped; and they deserve to be defeated or taken advantage of because they are wrong. In the more extreme case, a person might develop the belief that they have an obligation, maybe even a sacred mission, to deliver "justice" by punishing those who are weak or stupid enough to be susceptible to it (and who thus deserve it).

For a more "philosophical" argument, a person who despises laziness or stagnation above all else could point to exerting power, and especially exerting power over other people, as the antithesis of the ineffectual and inactive person, and could describe the violent way as the optimal way of living. It's possible to formulate a justification in this way, but no one is likely to seriously adopt this kind of philosophy unless they already had within them the desire to inflict violence on others, or to control people with the threat of violence, in the first place. Or, of course, a nonviolent person could attach themselves to it as a sort of philosophical role-play, if they like the aesthetics of conquest and adventure.

The frightening thing about the desire to exert power is that the person holding this desire, and having no awareness of any reason to inhibit it, can commit atrocities not just out of willful ignorance, as a bureaucrat following orders, but even out of something like *innocence,* as a small child pulling the legs off a spider. To have the power to kill or torture a living thing, and to exert this power out of simple curiosity and desire to play – yes, even a child is capable of this. How many adults have never grown out of this phase, but have simply gotten smarter, better, and more practiced at playing this game with their fellow human beings, whenever they should have one in the palm of their hand?

Those who are less inclined towards exerting power over others might well wonder why those belligerent warmongers can't simply mind their own business and stop invading other countries. Meanwhile, those more inclined towards it might well wonder why those apathetic good-for-nothings have so little interest in defending the good and righteous, and fighting against the forces of evil. Both personality types can be framed as a rationalization of one's past violent actions, or lack thereof. Like every other obsession and ideology, it all comes back to the development of morals via rationalization.

AWE

Religious ideology, also called dogma, is another type that can be stimulated by emotional experiences, particularly awe. The grand architecture of a cathedral, the enchantment of classical music, the beauty of a painting, and art of exceptional quality in any other medium (e.g. literature, oration, dance) can bring forth an overwhelming feeling of complete immersion, complete fixation, which is impossible to ignore. Outside of the realm of art, a good look at the right landscape, sunrise, or clear night sky can have the same effect; if a person is in the right mood, even something as small as the sight of a bee pollinating a flower could do the job, or an even smaller event. All of these things are sensations – and sensations can be brought on by plenty of things that are not divine.

From the sensation of awe, the preachers of dogma have an "in." A person who manages to capture another's attention by way of an awe-inducing experience has the ability to influence them, to take advantage of their immersed state of mind – to convince them that, since they can recognize this awe-inspiring event as being real, that there are other very real and very consequential things that they *must* attend to. "This magnificence could only have been created through divine inspiration; I wish to do the appropriate, respectful thing, and live in accordance with whatever produced this" – this is the desired sentiment. A question immediately follows: "What must I do to bring myself to a state of proper alignment, or grace?" The preachers of dogma pounce on this, and are happy to teach their catechism to those who are willing to listen. But are their teachings infallible? Do these codes of conduct and mandated beliefs actually lead to some kind of good outcome, let alone the *only* good outcome? It's tempting for the new convert to constantly keep that initial attracting factor, that feeling of experiencing something magnificent, something "transcendental," in the forefront of their mind, and submit entirely to whatever seems to have granted that pleasurable feeling. As discussed earlier, it's also tempting (for some people) to look for something to submit to *in general*, just for the sake of being granted a simple and clear path forward in life. But one must always be realistic. There is nothing wrong with experiencing awe as a reaction to great beauty – but you must be very careful not to sacrifice what you truly are to something that you merely feel. A dogmatist could use the opportunity given by awe to teach literally anything, good or evil or a mix of the two – there is nothing that prevents this from happening, so you must always keep a critical eye open, and never fall into the temptation to completely abandon your judgment, to abandon your soul, so to speak.

In the essay "Of Superstition and Enthusiasm," David Hume describes religious perspectives that can occur as projections of both positive and negative emotional conditions, which could in turn arise from any earthly cause – but the individual may not recognize the mundane origin of these sensations. From the one kind, "infinite unknown evils are dreaded from unknown agents...whose power and malevolence [the imagination] sets no limits," and from the other kind, "raptures, transports, and surprising flights of fancy...being altogether unaccountable, and seeming quite beyond the reach of our ordinary faculties, are attributed to the immediate inspiration of that Divine Being." Hume also speaks more generally about the projecting phenomenon in his excellent *Enquiry Concerning Human Understanding*. For example: "The idea of God, as meaning an infinitely intelligent, wise, and good Being, arises from reflecting on the operations of our own mind, and augmenting, without limit, those qualities of goodness and wisdom." This short and elegant book of his is essential reading for anyone with any interest in philosophy.

Based on the ubiquitous emergence of religion across all kinds of early human civilizations, there's a case to be made that there was some kind of substantial use to it, at some time in the past at least, and that it was beneficial to the species. There are probably elements of religion that are still beneficial today; but there are definitely elements present in all of today's most popular religions which are not beneficial. It is the task of the person who wants to be serious about their religious stance to separate the wheat from the chaff, to refuse any element of religion which either their conscience or their intellect cannot honestly tolerate.

Here is one example for monotheistic readers: Any person who is serious about their religious stance will find the concept of eternal damnation to be a strange one. To punish a dead person is strange, and to punish them eternally is even stranger. On Earth, punishment is given by human beings to other human beings (and animals, etc.) in order to discourage them from doing something. That is the very essence of the concept of punishment. But from what are the dead being discouraged? Will the sinful dead jump out of their graves and keep causing trouble if they're not properly disciplined? This is not even a question of being just or unjust; punishing the dead is downright nonsensical. The very concept of "punishment" is irrelevant when applied to the dead, unless some theory of reincarnation is involved – in which case, it can only be temporary punishment anyway, and the case could be made that the person is not really "dead." But even if it was the case that some kind of punishment was (for some reason) necessary to inflict on those who did evil deeds in life, what possible good could result from that punishment being infinite in length? Would it not be better for the condemned person, even the worst person in the world, to be transformed somehow into a good person, or at least given the opportunity to do so? And all this is not to speak of the equally absurd belief that such punishment would have something to do with God, the Supreme Being, stooping to the very petty human emotion of *being offended*. How, then, did eternal damnation as a concept come about? Like so many other ideological beliefs, the roots are simple. The fear of being eternally punished by a divine authority is a projection of social fears concerning punishment from earthly authorities: Parents, kings, priests, and so on. These human authorities can be offended (specifically, on occasions when something threatens or surpasses their ability to control things – a condition inaccessible to an omnipotent God), and these human authorities do give out punishments. It's easy to combine the permanence of death with the expectation of punishment and reward to yield this strange belief; but the strangeness of it can be detected merely by asking simple, obvious questions. And there's one more reason for the proliferation of such beliefs: those who are sadistic enough to relish the thought of their earthly opposition being tortured indefinitely in Hell. The desire for violence, too, can be projected into realms of eternity. "As above, so below; as below, so above": thus runs the quintessential superstition.

FALSE DICHOTOMY

Not uncommonly, the preachers of ideology will present to their audience a false dichotomy, an impression that, for such-and-such moral issue or policy question, there exists a very limited set of options that each person "has to" choose from. This makes it an easier task to convince a person of an ideology – if a person can be convinced that there are no other options besides selecting one of a few competing ideologies, then one of the major hurdles in the preaching of ideology (namely, convincing a person that they have to choose an ideology in the first place) is sidestepped. A person presents the world as a battle between two ideologies; with persuasive enough rhetoric, one ideology can be presented as totally unacceptable and the opposite can be presented as "flawed, but acceptable in comparison." If the preacher is feeling bolder, perhaps the ideology they are peddling could even be passed off as infallible.

For ideologies that concern today's most hotly-debated topics, the issues in question are likely to be very complex and difficult to reason about – if a fundamental question about public policy, for example, has existed for decades or centuries and is still disputed to this day, what does that say about how simple of a task it is to answer it? It's not impossible that a complex and difficult question might have a simple answer, but this would be rare. Nonetheless, the temptation to perceive the world in simple terms leads people to assume that all questions that can be asked in simple terms can be answered in simple terms.

False dichotomies prey on naïve people, especially young people, who still conceive of the world in simple yes-or-no terms, who have not yet started to treat complex questions with nuance. Nuance, indeed, is exactly what is not allowed in a false dichotomy: a person must pledge allegiance to one side or the other, no exceptions, no qualifications, no provisos. "If you're not with us, you must be one of *them*." Public intellectuals, pundits, government officials, and other high-visibility individuals will often be ridiculed for switching sides or even shifting their opinion slightly; any thought that would compel a person to abandon one ideology in favor of another, or in favor of a non-ideological stance, is discouraged. What is the message that a spectator is likely to take away, after observing this pattern again and again? That a person must select an absolutely correct choice on their first shot at forming an opinion, and that they must stick with this choice forever? If changing opinions is off the table, is it even possible to form an opinion, to think meaningfully about an opinion being right or wrong at all? Is the optimally "informed" person someone who selected an opinion and maintained it for their whole life, without once critically analyzing any aspect of it? This loyal character would indeed be the dream customer of whoever has something to gain by peddling an ideology.

False dichotomies can also be disguised as one side arguing truth, morality, or some other such absolutely correct thing, against falsehood, immorality, etc. This creates the illusion that the issue is not actually an ideological one. To avoid this, it's always useful to pay attention to the bottom line of what a person is arguing for: is this "truth" some kind of unverifiable metaphysical claim? Is this "moral" system that they've come up with something that actually makes sense, or is it just the rhetoric of a well-spoken person who is making a bid for popular support? Asking these questions can reveal whether such issues are actually ideological in nature. There are also red flags that can be detected in the methods of those who are preaching this so-called non-ideological issue: Do they use a lot of emotional, inciteful language? Are they making a profit from the people they convert, especially in the short term? Do they seem unwilling to address certain topics directly, instead steering the conversation so that they can say a particular catchphrase or soundbite, something that sounds good out of context? There are many ways to see that an issue advertised as "good versus evil" or "truth versus lies" is actually an ideological one. It's easy to get confused because some of the preachers of ideology have power and influence on a national, even global, scale; many people tend to equate authority with legitimacy, even while these very bastions of power tell you to "question authority" in so many words.

Interestingly, even if a person is ideologically possessed, it's often easy for them to spot the telltale signs of ideological possession in others – as long as these others support an opposing ideology. It's not uncommon to see two opposing ideologically-motivated parties arguing with each other, with both sides *simultaneously and correctly* accusing the other of being a mere follower of ideology, a brainwashed sheep or what have you, while steadily ignoring their own ideological hangups. Let that sink in: both sides correctly see the faults in the other's ideology, but not in their own, sometimes even when the faults in both sides are of the very same type. A neutral person, observing such an argument without personal involvement, should be able to learn the faults of both parties, and come to a more nuanced conclusion of their own on whatever topic is at hand.

Similarly, consider how popular it is for large organizations, especially political parties, to try to adopt the aesthetic of the rebel. You don't need to watch a news program for more than a few minutes before seeing a talking head referring to his political party of choice as, one way or another, rebelling against "the system" with which the opposing political party is oppressing the public. This is true regardless of which slant the news program in question takes. In reality, both major parties (in a two-party system) will be happy to identify the opposing side as supporting "the system," but fail to admit that their own side also supports the same system, or rather, is a part of this system. Government officials worth hundreds of millions of dollars will complain about both the rich *and* the government. You can buy a "Better Dead Than Red" sticker that's made in a Communist nation, and you can buy an "Eat the Rich" t-shirt from a website owned by a billionaire. The aesthetic of the rebel is just that, an aesthetic, which can be adopted at a moment's notice, even by the most firmly-established powers of the world, and at the moment, it seems to be doing a very good job of convincing supporters of the establishment that they are somehow opposing it. Be careful not to fall for it.

Beware, also, of any situation where you feel pressured into choosing one thing or the other – especially quickly, without time to think. A tense moment in the middle of a conversation is no setting to form an opinion. Don't be afraid to say "I don't know" or even "I don't care," if that's the truth. If you hastily choose yes or no, if you pigeonhole yourself, if you categorize your identity all of a sudden, you may afterwards feel like there are certain things you "have to" do in order to fit in, to retain consistency, to not look stupid, because you're now "in that category." This is one of the most significant dangers of ideology: the sorting of people into simple categories, with no nuance allowed. This is no way to proceed in developing a personal identity, nor personal opinions on policy issues, social issues, or any other such thing. This ideological trap is what brings people to choose a "side," and to agree with that "side" rather than simply thinking for themselves. The bait of this trap is the illusion that, by making such a choice, by putting themselves into such a box, the person *is* thinking for themselves. It's a very tempting bait, because it's devilishly hard for a person to differentiate organically-formed opinions from hastily-made opinions that they've simply rationalized after putting themselves into a box. A technique to differentiate these will be detailed in Part IV.

FANTASIES OF PERSECUTION

Another weapon of the ideological recruiter is the fantasy of being persecuted. It's a fantasy story ubiquitous to humanity, the story of the victim overcoming the oppressor, the underdog victory, the person who started with nothing achieving greatness in the face of adversity. Naturally, many people will be attracted to that kind of fantasy and will like to imagine themselves in that role, as the oppressed victim – whether they are actually an oppressed victim or not. A person actually being victimized identifying with this role is not necessarily a problem, and it may well encourage them to overcome the difficulties they face in life; the real issue occurs when a person starts thinking of themselves as a victim, contrary to the facts of their privileged situation. A method of pigeonholing one's identity, a denial of reality, a framing of the world in simple terms: this phenomenon is the seed of no small number of ideological issues.

The temptation to conceptualize oneself as a victim can arise from more unsavory inclinations than the desire to overcome one's actual oppressed situation. Some people wish to place themselves in that role in order to acquire (or at least role-play as having acquired) the privilege of being underprivileged: as it is permanently fashionable to help the underprivileged and listen to their complaints, the person who adopts the victim role can find (in those people who will listen to them) a free pass to complain frequently, to be judgmental, and perhaps even to personally demand things from others. The effectiveness of this tactic depends on how tolerant this person's audience is for such behavior; some will notice that the apparent victim is actually living a very privileged life and is in no position to speak as one of the underprivileged, let alone speak for a population of them (e.g., on social issues).

On the other hand, there is also the primitive comfort of futility, the tranquility that a person can afford by simply accepting that they are a victim, that there is nothing that they can do to change their circumstances, and that they therefore don't have to bother exerting any physical or mental energy to change things – since "changing things would be impossible," they say to themselves. This danger is liable to affect people who are being genuinely victimized, and the temptation it offers makes it even more difficult for a person to escape from such a position; but it can affect the privileged in a similar way. Human beings are very adaptive, and they can tolerate a very deprived way of life; some people, subconsciously aware of this fact, are confident enough in their own ability to survive that they adopt a masochistic desire to remain at the bottom of the ladder, so to speak, to be someone permanently ineffectual, to remain a nobody, and to tell themselves that they will forever remain a nobody. Such people as this will probably find themselves tormented by their conscience from time to time, by their knowledge that they could become more than what they are, that they do not have to remain a nobody, that they are capable of becoming greater. While the desire to maintain the status quo is strong, also strong is the desire to exert one's power onto the world.

A person who finds themselves thinking frequently about their own status as a victim (in whatever sense: economic, social, etc.) should try to step back now and again, and take a mental inventory of their life, asking themselves, "What do I actually have going for me in this life? How good do I actually have it? What am I actually capable of?" Even the severely underprivileged may find that they have certain advantages on their side; if nothing else, there is the willingness of others to help the underprivileged that they could rely on – if they can be humble enough to ask for help, and have the integrity and discernment to use what is given to its fullest potential. As this victim complex is a very common proto-ideological mental trap, you should not be embarrassed if you happen to find that you have fallen for it. Get it over with: acknowledge the fact of it, dedicate yourself to changing, change, and move on to better things.

STRANGE INTERSECTION

There is a strange intersection between a few apparently unrelated ideology-adjacent areas of thought: social conservatism, mystical/religious/superstitious thought, and conspiracy theorism. One way that the correlation between these ideas can be explained is by examining the types of emotional motivations, the personal tastes, which are projected into ideological beliefs on these subjects. The pertinent motivations are the idealization of the past and an affinity towards making generalizations.

Social conservatism idealizes the past by insisting that the moral concepts of the past should be perpetuated, especially concerning the law. This is correlated with religion by the simple historical fact of religious thought having dominated law and morality for thousands of years. But where do the ideas of conspiracy come in? Consider what it means to idealize the past. If the people of the past were intelligent and strong, how could the people of the present have become stupid and weak? How could the strong be defeated by the weak? Only an intelligent force could orchestrate such a thing; some group of intelligent people must have betrayed the rest of intelligent society and orchestrated this whole collapse in secret. And they probably did this in order to produce a weak global population that they alone would control from the shadows, et cetera, et cetera. If you insist on believing in an idealized version of the past, this quintessential conspiracy theory emerges as one of the simplest possible explanations.

Of course, to idealize the past is a misguided way of thinking in general, and it is likely a result of receiving limited information: history's villains aside, almost all of the individuals of the past who we learn about (particularly in school, and also in popular culture) are highly influential people, exceptionally good examples of humanity, whose achievements have made it into the history books. If you do not think very carefully about what you're reading, you may come to believe that *all* of the people of the past were these paragons of virtue, that the people then were simply better than the people of today. But the average Joe of antiquity was almost certainly as opportunistic, stupid, and mean as the average Joe of today, if not worse. The kings and plutocrats of the past were as brutal and greedy as the world leaders and billionaires of today, if not worse. Even the most praised figures of the past, due to the environment in which they were raised, often had a moral compass that would be considered intolerably cruel, or accepting of oppressive systems, by today's standards, however progressive they were for their time. Indeed, though our planet and our society still have a great deal of extremely serious problems, almost everything seems to have improved over time, and much of this is owed to the efforts of those who revolted against the restrictive policies and traditions of the past. And who would be foolish enough to say that all of those past revolutions were fine, but no future revolutions are allowed? A surprising number of conservatives will say so.

One other potential factor in this phenomenon is the projection of nostalgia, the sentimentality towards one's personal past, to a broader romanticization of the past in general. Many people perceive their childhood as a time of being protected (by their parents), a time with scarcely any knowledge of the evils of the world, an optimistic time as a whole; especially compared with the far more stressful times of adolescence and adulthood, into both of which one finds oneself abruptly shoved. If the idea of "the past was better" is stuck in one's mind based on personal experience, and especially if one still idolizes one's parents (or any other older authority figure, i.e., one associated with the past), making the leap to imagine a utopian past is not at all difficult. This may be manifested in an ideological sense as an insistent belief in some mythology or alternate history theory featuring a utopian prehistorical state of humanity, or as some sort of conservative ideological tendency, such as Luddism. In a non-ideological obsessive sense, many people preoccupy themselves with attempts to "return to childhood" in diverse ways, often very transparently.

The second point of intersection is an affinity towards making generalizations, and in particular, *insisting* upon adherence to generalizations. Merely making generalizations is not necessarily what you would call ideological in and of itself, though it can be a hindrance to developing an open-minded perspective. To go even further, and insist upon adhering to a generalization, is to remain completely closed-minded: to jump from the claim of "most things are this way" to "everything should be this way," and from "most people do this" to "everyone must do this." A willingness to make this kind of logical leap is a projection of the assumption that whatever the status quo is must be good, an assumption that many people hold subconsciously due to the tendency to equilibrium. This is directly related to conservative social thought for obvious reasons. It is also linked to religious and mystical thought by the premise that there is some kind of "natural order" to the world, common in the past if not the present, concerning which God (or nature, or something) will reward adherence and punish deviance. Conspiracy theorism is not so tightly tied to this concept; however, one-dimensional readings of people and of groups of people (e.g., framing historical figures and groups as simply "the good guys" or "the bad guys") make past and present events easy to frame in the context of a conspiracy theory-esque narrative. Indeed, simplicity in general makes such narratives easier to digest for the person who is frustrated at the world, but who doesn't want to put too much effort into figuring out the real nature of the issues.

To elaborate on the notion of "natural order," or sometimes "natural law," it's interesting to note that there are many people (often, you will notice, of a vindictive or judgmental persuasion) who would insist that it is the duty of a human effort (such as the government) to punish some behavior that they deem to be "unnatural." Now, if this behavior is something that harms another person in a manner recognized by the law, the law will take action regardless of the "unnatural" nature of the crime. But what if this unnatural act is only detrimental to the person performing it? Again, if a person is tangibly harming themselves somehow, the government can intervene; but only sometimes, and typically in a protective rather than a punitive sense (it's not illegal to become an alcoholic, but there are government-subsidized rehab centers). But some people would insist that certain "unnatural" behaviors, which are not evidently self-harm and which are not harmful to others, should be against the law. An obvious question arises: if the thing is "unnatural" in the sense that it violates some "natural law," the implication being that something will "naturally" punish those who do these things, why is human enforcement necessary at all? If the detrimental effects of this unnatural thing are so easily manifest, then it's bound to fall out of popularity, no? Or at the very least, pertinent information about its detriments will become widespread. Scientific articles will be written that show the relationship between the thing and its negative effect, just as surely as such articles have already been written about nicotine, alcohol, lead paint, asbestos insulation, and chlorofluorocarbons. The law may even prohibit certain things if the harm is determined to be frequent and severe enough. But this determination has to be made by the consensus of the pertinent scientific community, at minimum. If the thing in question is not detrimental enough to convince those who study such things for a living, then to call it categorically bad is a statement of opinion at best, regardless of where this theory of this "natural law" might have originated.

OPPOSITE INTERSECTION

Let's also talk about the opposite of the behaviors discussed in the previous section: the idealization of change and an affinity against generalizations. Again, these ideas are not themselves problematic, but to project them onto one's opinions about the world at large can lead a person to unrealistic ideological inclinations.

Idealization of change, when carried to an ideological degree, becomes an insistence that whatever the status quo is must be bad and must be changed. Granted, since no status quo is perfect in every way, there will always be some conceivable positive change on the horizon. There is even a case to be made that the people cannot (and thus, should not) ever be completely satisfied, and that no matter what happens in the future, we should always be on the lookout for the next beneficial change we can make to society, and to constantly work towards the next improvement. The type to be ideologically obsessed about this, though, is the type to instantly lock onto every non-issue that seems tangentially related to social change, to make explosive statements about it, and in general to treat every microscopic violation as if it's an issue of paramount importance. This is counterproductive because it detracts attention from actual social issues, and because it gives a bad name to those actually working in pursuit of improved social conditions. Another type of ideologue in this category, probably less common, is the type to outright advocate or commit violence, where it is not warranted or useful, in the name of some fashionable moral claim for social progress. This is also counterproductive, for obvious reasons.

The inclination to refuse generalizations is a reasonable one, but, like any other inclination, it can be carried too far. This can occur in a few different ways. For one, if a generalization has some kind of basis in a well-established fact, a person could deny this fact solely for the sake of posturing against the generalization. Alternately (or perhaps concurrently), a person might insist upon a generalization that is the opposite of the "mainstream" generalization; but this new generalization could be easily as misguided and harmful as the original, or worse. These kinds of attitudes are pure contrarianism, and are related to the aesthetic of the rebel, the desire to be different or in opposition to the mainstream (or something they consider "mainstream" – after all, some people consider themselves rebels because they stand against opinions that haven't been popular since their grandparents' generation) just for the sake of it. There are plenty of things in this world that are self-evidently worth opposing, and these things can be fought against without making the same type of overgeneralization that the political opposition makes.

There are also conspiracy theories that can be found intersecting with these ideological leanings, normally revolving around the concept of an ultra-powerful class of elites who behave much like cartoon supervillains, just to acquire money and maintain the status quo (i.e., the environment in which they can continue acquiring lots of money). Determining which conspiracies of this kind are real and which are fictitious is left as an exercise for the reader.

IDENTITY ORGANIZATION

A person who has pigeonholed themselves can decide to adopt an ideological stance, or join an ideological group, without thinking about it. This is troublesome for two reasons. First, it's nonsensical to decide on a label for yourself without knowing what the label means or whether it actually applies to you. It's dishonest to call yourself by a certain label, or declare your allegiance to a certain group, without knowing what it is you're actually declaring. Second, in the likely scenario that what you've declared about yourself is not accurate, it's easy to feel pressured to remain in that group regardless, and betray your own interests for the contrary interests of the group, by several forces: post-hoc rationalization, peer pressure, pressure from authority figures, and the propaganda of whatever ideology is relevant to the group. If you don't understand what a group stands for, it's best to wait, and avoid these issues, rather than rush immediately into complete personal investment.

To avoid ideological attachment, it's important to bear certain basic principles in mind. If you find yourself a part of a group, you are not obligated to remain in that group permanently. There is no need to call yourself something that you are not, or say something that you do not believe. And if there are people who you consider to be your friends pressuring you into saying things you don't believe, or doing things you don't want – these people are no friends of yours. Friends don't tell friends to lie. Friends don't tell friends to betray their consciences. This is assuming, of course, that you are not being physically coerced into it by something like a tyrannical government or abusive parents – if this is the case, my condolences and I wish you the best of luck in escaping.

Granted, there are certain things that can only be learned by trying them out, by diving into an idea or belief to understand what it is. Kids, especially, will spontaneously try out personality traits, beliefs, and all kinds of other things by imitation, in order to learn what works and what doesn't. Sometimes, they'll deliberately say things that are contrary to what some adult says, just to see what happens. I distinctly remember that when I was about 5, I had an argument with my dad, since I had become convinced that the speed of sound was faster than the speed of light. What had convinced me? Nothing. A whim. Why did I believe this? No real reason, not even out of some conscious desire to rebel or make fun, but just because I could. Why not? At that time, choosing one fact over another was no different than choosing a favorite color, especially a fact so distant and difficult to demonstrate. Kids can be forgiven for this, but adults are generally assumed to have more developed brains. Adults should be able to form opinions without diving headfirst into something, without completely investing their identity into a trope or stereotype, an image of a group or ideology.

Suppose that a few people from a church youth group get together and decide to make a Christian rock band. They decide to play Christian rock before they've played a single note together, or before any of them have decided on what instrument to play, for that matter. Do you see something wrong with this picture? If they haven't played any music, how do they know what kind of music they actually want to dedicate themselves to? If they place this label on themselves beforehand, everything that they play together afterwards will have to be filtered through their interpretation of the category "Christian rock." I suspect that a lot of Christian rock bands form in this very way, and I suspect that this is directly related to why so much of the genre is so lame and unimaginative, even compared to the proportion that Sturgeon's Law would predict. Would it not be better to play the kind of music that you're good at, and the kind of music that you like, and then decide on what genre to call it afterwards, in order to avoid any bias or unnecessary restriction going in? The most inspired musicians are often called "genre-defying," which is not surprising given that the opposite of imitation is innovation. Whoever is able to create art without imitating existing tropes has more freedom as an artist, and has the potential to create greater art.

So it goes with matters of opinion. Don't be hasty with categorizing yourself. You can say that you like one ideology or category or political party more than another, without investing yourself in it. Don't be hasty with calling yourself this or that, especially if the terms involved can lead to confusion – one man's Christian is another man's atheist, and one man's moderate is another man's radical. With the power of the Internet, you can research beliefs and ideologies without the personal investment (and risk) of intensively trying them out. Decide for yourself what your beliefs are first, and let any categorization wait until later.

LIMBO OF BELIEF

A person can think one thing and do another, or do something without thinking at all; the way that a person thinks is important, but it is their words and actions which are ultimately consequential. It's not difficult to find examples of people who cling wholeheartedly to an ideology without appearing to do any thinking on the topic whatsoever. If a person does not think about what it is that they do, it's hard to say whether they truly "believe" in what they do, or what they say, even to themselves. If a person says that they believe in something, and acts as if they believe in something, but they don't know a thing about this issue that they say they have an opinion on, and the actions taken toward this belief don't have any thought put into them – is their "belief" really a belief?

Let's clarify how this kind of behavior might come about. As explained in earlier sections, people act spontaneously, without thinking, especially children. It's beneficial that they do this, because it enables them to learn the consequences of a variety of behaviors. Of course, it also leads to some strange situations. A middle-schooler will pick up curse words and dirty phrases from their classmates, movies, or the Internet, and spontaneously start using them *before they know what they mean.* Why? If you ask a small child why they do something unusual, they'll probably say "I don't know." When the kid gets a little older and a little smarter, they'll say something like "I thought it would be funny." Interesting phrase, isn't it? "I thought it would be funny." A kid sees a clip of a stand-up comedian giving a one-liner about drugs or sex or something, and getting a laugh. The kid doesn't get the joke, but sees that it got a laugh. And so, the kid repeats the phrase to his friends the next day, without knowing what the words mean. Odds are low that the kid was really thinking very hard about when and where to deploy the new phrase; he just wanted to try it out, "because it would be funny." The kid later learns what it was that he said to his friends that day and why they gave him a weird look for saying it, and he cringes at the memory. His inclination to spout that phrase off at random is inhibited.

As people grow up, the development of their mind causes their behavior to become more inhibited – in certain areas. That is, the areas wherein it seems useful for their behavior to be inhibited. In other areas, where the person feels that they can get away with being uninhibited, the state of being uninhibited remains by default, and actions will continue to emerge spontaneously. A grown adult does something absolutely outrageous in public and acts as if it's completely normal – why? It's not because they think it's "the right thing to do." In fact, they're probably not thinking about what's right or wrong in this situation at all. Instead, it's because they literally have not learned to inhibit this part of themselves, this part that "wants" to do this behavior, so to speak, from simply acting spontaneously. In other cases, it could be alcohol, or some other drug, that caused the person to become more uninhibited overall. Additionally, the person in question will sometimes even be *offended* when they are treated by others as someone who has done something outrageous; once again, the thought that their behavior in this kind of situation should be more inhibited simply did not occur to them, and perhaps has never occurred to them.

Any sort of behavior could be subject to this same phenomenon, this spontaneous action due to lack of inhibition. How about those behaviors associated with ideological fixation? What if a person acts uninhibited in such a way that the end result is one-to-one identical with a person ideologically possessed, or otherwise obsessed with a particular idea or pattern of behavior? This happens all the time. In an ordinary conversation, a person instantly becomes enraged when a certain topic is broached, and starts ranting about their opinion. Why? Because they never learned not to react this way. A person sees a headline, and instantly, at the first opportunity, tells all their friends about it, swearing up and down that the event in question (as interpreted by this person from the one sentence that the headline consisted of) is both critically important and absolutely factual as described. Why? Because they never learned to inhibit the flow of information from headline to mouth.

This leads to a weird consequence: it is possible to adopt an ideological stance for no reason, for the same lack of reason that a kid might justify after the fact by saying "I thought it would be funny." But for something as serious as an ideological attachment, adults don't have recourse to this childish justification. The most common similar statement would be "Well, it's just what I believe." Funnily enough, this is actually an even worse defense. The former identifies the potential for humor as an actual reason for wanting to do something. The latter essentially doesn't communicate anything other than "I did it because it's the kind of thing I do." The word "belief" can be used to mean so much, or so little! This state of ambiguity, this situation where a person makes statements or takes action while their conscious level of "belief" in these statements or actions is ambiguous, is the limbo of belief.

What kind of ideas might be acquired in this naïve way, and later fermented into ideological stances? What is it that has that attractive, "funny" factor? The outlandish, for one, is always attractive. Anything contrary to popular thought has the automatic appeal of the different, the new, the daring. A person can make an entire career out of doing outlandish things, saying outrageous things, upsetting lots of people, and putting on the aesthetic of the unaffected, cool outsider. This character, the one who is capable of doing that which is not allowed, is instantly attractive to a certain audience; it seems to them as if he is able to do the impossible, break the barriers of society's expectations, be a genuine rebel against the system, etc. It's easy to get caught up, obsessing over this charismatic image, and not care too much about what the person is actually doing and saying. It's easy to want to imitate such a character, and be so preoccupied that you neglect to consider the bottom line: what is it that you actually want to do here? Is imitating this person actually going to result in you moving closer to the life you actually want, or are you merely a child imitating a cartoon character? Is it possible, despite this character seeming so cool and superior to you, that imitating him is actually a terrible idea and would only bring your life to injury? It's very possible that this character's life is only a façade, not anything real, but merely a show that he can put on under certain conditions. Could it be that you are deliberately ignoring things he's done or said, things that you dislike or cannot justify, to maintain this image of perfection, this hero-worship, in your head? It's very tempting to excuse the faults (even very serious faults) of the people whom you want to like. But if you're not willing to think critically about this person, it's not even really accurate to say that you like him; only that you've been fooled into acting like you like him. Those who think they've discovered a perfect individual will always be disappointed.

Interestingly, the attractive factor of an attitude being novel, different, contrary, is not limited to attitudes associated with the seeking-out of *more* freedom. When the status quo is to celebrate liberty and encourage openness, conservatism and restriction acquire something sort of similar to the air of rebellion: the air of the immovable rock that remains solid amidst swirling chaos. This is the aesthetic of the monk, the character who obtains exceptional wisdom, or whatever other desirable trait, by means of strict limitations placed on their life, to the exclusion of a large number of what are considered "normal" activities. It is possible to find oneself in the limbo of belief, and to move toward this kind of lifestyle, imitating it and investing precious time in it, without thinking carefully about what it actually entails. It is possible to be attracted toward it, due to its aesthetic, when it is not actually what you want. It is possible to fool yourself into adopting a monastic lifestyle, and to spend such a long time repeating the relevant rites and practicing so many forms of abstinence that the result becomes your new equilibrium; and you may find yourself trapped in a prison of your own creation, which you despise but feel attached to nonetheless – because you built it.

And inversely, for those who prefer something more chaotic, there is also the aesthetic of the radical. A person can be tempted, through aesthetic means or otherwise, into sowing chaos wherever they go, perhaps more chaos than is actually appropriate to reach the results that they want. There are many useful objectives in life that are severely hindered, if not rendered impossible, by a life burdened by a reputation for destruction and disorderliness, especially a life with a criminal record. If any of these objectives in life are part of what you want, then what you want could be destroyed by carelessly biting off more chaos than you can chew, while acting spontaneously within the limbo of belief.

Allowing your beliefs to become muddled in this way, in this kind of limbo, emerging from you in practice but not being present in your thoughts, can cause you to wake up one morning and find you're stuck in a life that you don't want, but which simply seemed to envelop itself around you – because you never took the time to think about what you wanted and what you didn't want.

POE'S LAW

An important concept, related to the above ambiguity of belief, is Poe's Law, which states that satire, unless very clearly identified by the speaker as satire, is indistinguishable from sincerity. A person makes a hyperbolic statement that *could* be a comical impression of such-and-such ideological opinion; it *could* be that this person is making a joke, but on the other hand, people with such-and-such ideological opinion are known to say the same exact thing from time to time. Without context, the statement is not clearly identifiable as either sincere expression of a ridiculous opinion, or satire of the same.

This is not limited to satirical statements about others. A person might make an exaggerated statement which is a more extreme version of their (presumable) actual beliefs, as a joke. But if it's not entirely clear that they're joking, how can their audience interpret it? At Thanksgiving dinner, an uncle who is known to be wary of mainstream news suddenly starts talking about news networks being controlled by some kind of conspiracy, and says it in a way that seems silly enough that it *could* be self-satire...but is it? An awkward pause ensues. Someone asks, "Are you messing around or are you serious?" He replies "I'm serious, it's the truth." But this could still be part of a satirical joke. He's questioned a little more, and seems to hold his position until someone changes the subject. Could it be that he was joking the whole time? No one really knows. It's possible that not even the uncle himself knows.

Recall the key phrase "I thought it would be funny." It's possible for a person to say something spontaneously, without actually having a real opinion on whether the words they're saying are true or not, sincere or satire. Given a bad reaction, a person could play nearly any such spontaneous statement off as a joke, and pretend that it was meant to be satire from the start. And wouldn't those accusers look silly, taking a mere joke so seriously? And after being made to look like fools who can't tell a joke from a serious claim, maybe those accusers won't be so quick to question outlandish claims when they come up in the future. This is advantageous to anyone in the habit of making such claims, for any reason (or lack of reason). It's possible for a comedian, for example, to make extreme-sounding claims, and to take advantage of Poe's Law to keep their real position totally ambiguous: either they truly believe it and are only making it seem like it could be satire, or they are truly performing satire and are only making it seem like it could be sincere, or they could be in the limbo of belief, not having a true opinion whatsoever, but only having an interest in getting a certain kind of response from the audience.

To cite a well-known example of satire being indistinguishable from sincerity, consider Kurt Vonnegut's 1961 short story *Harrison Bergeron.* It's possible for a person to read it as just what it appears to be on the surface, a darkly-comical warning against unnatural and hamfisted means of producing a state of equality. It's possible to read it as just that, and completely ignore the fact that it's actually a satire of *Atlas Shrugged,* which had been published four years prior. It's pretty obvious satire too, what with the villains using the most cartoonishly brute-force means of enforcing their agenda, with success and talent being punished explicitly, and Bergeron being the hyperbolically powerful and egoistic hero, even whimsically declaring himself emperor. The anticlimactic execution of this superman by way of a shotgun (Rand's protagonists never die) is the icing on the satirical cake. I just lied to your face. Did you believe those last few sentences? In reality, there's no evidence whatsoever that *Harrison Bergeron* was intended by the author to be anything other than a straightforward warning against excessive government intervention with public life. Vonnegut's comments on the short story's citation in a 2005 court case reinforce the straightforward reading, as does the fact that the self-handicapping concept had previously occurred (again in a straightforward context, in the sense of not satirizing another author) in his novel *The Sirens of Titan.* This is a shame, because *Harrison Bergeron* is actually a lot funnier when it's read as a Rand parody. Anyway, the fact that it can be read as such demonstrates that the converse of Poe's Law is also true: just as satire can be mistaken for sincerity, sincerity can also be mistaken for satire. There are undoubtedly many celebrated authors and playwrights (especially satirists) from previous centuries whose views are so foreign to ours that we might mistake their earnest statements for satirical ones; and, to make things even more complicated, they could hypothetically be either satirical of what was then the mainstream view, *or* of a view that was at the time considered radical. A few hundred years ago, the most commonplace opinions on politics, race, gender relations, sexual morality, and numerous other topics would be considered today to be unreasonably intolerant. An opinion once considered common sense (perhaps even *factual*, not even a matter of opinion) could be looked upon by a modern audience as so cartoonish that we would be tempted to say, "It simply must be a joke."

Lastly, Poe's Law can be a mechanism by which a person in the limbo of belief can be turned toward extremism, toward actual dangerous behaviors. Say that a person is in the habit of making certain "jokes," such as the "joke" told by the uncle a few paragraphs ago. A person who says such things, without actually thinking very hard about how serious they are about what they're saying, might find themselves coming to believe a literal (rather than comedic) interpretation of its contents. Tell enough self-deprecating jokes, for example, and you could plausibly start to sincerely hold a lower opinion of yourself. Surround yourself by enough people expressing a certain opinion and, by the mere-exposure effect, you may start to become more attracted to that opinion – and this is a risk no matter whether you're only in this environment (e.g., a social circle or an online forum) "as a joke," whether the people involved are only expressing these opinions "as a joke," or both, or neither. Jokes are humorous subversions of expectation. If the "joke" is something continuously expressed, no longer being unexpected, then it's one of two things: either a joke that has gotten stale, or something that is no longer a mere joke, and has turned into something serious.

EXERCISE IN OPEN-MINDEDNESS

One of the reasons why it's so difficult to separate yourself from an ideological belief, or any oversimplified view of things, is because you almost certainly assume that your beliefs are rational. Everybody does, because everybody makes rational judgments based on their past experiences, the things that they associate with right and wrong, effective and ineffective, logical and illogical, useful and useless. But this is obviously not a very robust assumption, because, as described earlier, these associations with right and wrong, rational or irrational, are not founded on some objective standpoint (as if any such thing exists), but on rationalizations – on the models and categorizations that are satisfactory for what an individual has dealt with so far in life. Once again: human beings, including you, are not rational animals. This is a fact that you must come to terms with if you intend to separate yourself from the sorts of ideologies that plague people, that make them see life through a tiny, narrow, restricted window. You may very well be looking at life through such a window right now and not even know it. But how is it possible to convince a person of such a thing? How can a person detect this in themselves? How can a "rational mind" come to recognize one of its own beliefs as irrational, when every belief it has was formed through means that compel it, through direct experience, to call those beliefs rational?

First, to demonstrate the principle of the thing, here are some examples of the essential irrationality of human beings in action. First of all, there are mass marketing, political campaigns, and other similar endeavors to appeal to people *en masse*. What are the most effective methods of appealing? Emotional ones, obviously, such as the instillation of fear and anger in order to stir up patriotism, religious zeal, and such; also, the presentation of characters (in advertisements, for example) in desirable social situations, and correlating these situations with the product to be sold or the idea to be marketed, preying on the emotions also responsible for peer pressure. Even certain sensations below the level of emotion, on the level of instinct, can be used for this purpose. The fact that sex sells is so obvious that it's barely worth repeating. The bright color schemes of fast-food corporations are used because they appeal to our ancestral attraction toward the bright colors of fruit. The direct consequence of this is that the majority of people can be, and very often are, swayed by arguments and images that are not what one would call "rational." Some commentators have used the term "post-truth" when they observe this effect on large populations today; but this is completely backwards. Our society is not post-truth, it's pre-truth. Our civilization is not yet advanced enough that rational arguments are more effective for swaying the opinion of the populace than emotional appeals – of course, part of the reason for this is because there's hardly any large-scale consensus as to what a rational argument actually, categorically, is. Different people and different groups have come to very different understandings about the world through their diverse rationalizations of their experiences. In contrast, the universality of certain styles of emotional appeal makes them easily powerful enough to render a much more consistent "consensus" agreement.

For a second example, reader, consider what kind of a person you were five years ago. It's very likely that, at that time, you said to yourself that you knew what you were talking about, that you understood certain things about the world, about right and wrong, about how people should be, what they should do and what they shouldn't do. How naïve you were back then, as five additional years of experience have no doubt shown! Of course, today, with the same amount of confidence, you still say to yourself that you know what you're talking about, and perhaps that's a more accurate statement. But are you, by any chance, treating it as if it were a *completely correct* statement? You may have separated yourself from certain bad ideas that you fell for back then, but are you perhaps under the delusion that you've immunized yourself from falling for bad ideas in general? What is it exactly that makes you think that none of your beliefs are stupid? Is it because you think that you're rational, and that in spite of all those other people who think they're rational but aren't, you actually are rational? Were you perhaps reading the previous paragraph thinking that it was referring to a category of person that includes almost everyone, but just so happens to exclude you?

When you understand the limitations of your rationality, when you understand that you cannot simply judge the world according to a very small set of "rational" rules, and when you realize and accept that you can be wrong, you will be much more capable of separating yourself from ideology, and you will have a more open, nuanced, and realistic perspective about the world and your place in it. You will find yourself less often "fundamentally disagreeing" with people to the point of frustration, you will less often totally exclude people's arguments from your consideration, because you will realize that it's interesting to hear and think about novel perspectives, even if they do turn out to be wrong. It's difficult to actually do this, but it can be done.

If you want to see a more specific illustration of this principle, try taking up chess. Play a few rated games a day online for several weeks at least (preferably against real people rather than AI), and analyze the games afterwards, if possible. You will make mistakes so stupid and so "irrational" that you will be appalled at yourself, wondering how a person who is not blind could make such obvious blunders. But that's the issue - you were blind, in those moments, because though you could see the pieces, and though you knew the rules of the game, you did not recognize the state of the board, or the moves that your opponent was likely to make. These kinds of recognitions cannot be learned until the mind feels an *incentive* to learn them - an incentive like avoiding the negative emotions associated with losing a game, for example. And such an incentive will only be recognized when it is reinforced through *practice,* through repetition of some action where the incentive is recalled. Conversely, information which is ostensibly easy to recall may wind up lost to oblivion if it is not the kind of information a person has an incentive to use - remembering the name and personal details of a person you've only met once, for example, doesn't have much incentive to it, unless there was something special and memorable about this encounter. The very notion of an event being "memorable" implies that an individual, or at least their subconscious mind, treats the memories gained, the information gained, as something expected to be useful for the future. This is the nature of learning. Bear in mind an important consequence of this - unless you have firsthand experience in a certain field, you are very likely missing important knowledge about it, and you may even be totally blind to its real nature. Imagine a chess novice who gets great entertainment out of watching other people play chess on the Internet, and who can follow the logic behind particular moves - after it is explained to them. This person could easily imagine that they're good at chess, because they "understand" these explanations - but they will be in for a rude awakening when they attempt to play some rated games online for the first time and discover just how much of a newbie they really are. In how many areas of life could you be blind in this same way, concerning the things that you pay attention to, comment on, and maybe even think you're "well-versed" in, while in reality only watching from a distance?

To phrase the above another way, methods of "rational thinking" might seem obvious when viewed from the outside, or after the fact, but they would *barely occur in a person's mind at all* in-the-moment until and unless specific experiences have imprinted the relevant information, and developed a method of determining what is "rational" and what is "irrational" given a certain scenario. Firsthand experience is absolutely essential to making a "rational" judgment, and so people are only actually capable of being strictly "rational" in the limited number of fields that they have firsthand experience working with. Still, people will constantly try to explore new fields, and extend their more general principles of "rational" problem-solving to areas they're not familiar with, which might work to some degree in some cases – but their judgment is by no means certain.

In general, reasonably intelligent and reasonably open-minded people will be expected to have the most success in this technique of extending the set of fields onto which they apply their system of rationality – but what about people who are not open-minded, or more specifically, what about people whose manner of "rational" thinking, which they consider rational and which (they believe) has worked for them perfectly well over the years, is not open-ended, but is very conceptually rigid and restrictive? If a person's thought process is limited by rules that they insist upon, and are not willing to budge on, there may be certain fields that they are unable to participate in in an effective ("rational") sense. For instance, there are some religious folks who believe absolutely adamantly, unquestionably, in whatever dogma it is that they subscribe to. Individuals in such a group can make convincing arguments to each other by referencing the dogma, since it's something that both parties consider to be fundamentally true. But a person in this group would have difficulty convincing someone outside of this group using the same sort of argument, the argument from dogma that they consider "rational" – because in order for an argument from dogma to be convincing, the listener has to *already* believe in the dogma. This difficulty of communication is the reason why dogma, and ideology in general, are obstacles to rational thought, and why people who become most egregiously obsessed with ideology are looked down upon – by those who are not themselves egregiously obsessed.

UNRELIABLE

Rationality is the rationalization of emotions, and emotions are the manifestations of instincts. Even morality can be described as an abstraction of rationality: That which is always preferable, from a rational perspective, is considered moral, and the opposite immoral; and nothing can be considered moral if it is not at minimum practical, that is, as judged from a rational perspective. The genealogy of all thought, however objective or pure it might seem to a person, can be traced to the most primitive functions of the human brain (and, in general, the body). In the opening pages of *Beyond Good and Evil*, Nietzsche writes: "By far the greater part of conscious thinking must still be included among instinctive activities, and that goes even for philosophical thinking...Most of the conscious thinking of a philosopher is secretly guided and forced into certain channels by his instincts." Why does Kafka's hunger artist make fasting into his entire career, his entire lifestyle, capturing the amazement of so many people? Because he could never find food that he likes.

The consequence of this is that one's ideas about the world can never be considered to be unquestionably trustworthy, one can never assume that one has arrived at the ultimate truth. There is no process by which "the truth" is handed to a person by some kind of ultimate authority, be it God or Reason or Science. Even our most solid ideas are, at their deepest and most fundamental level, constructions of simple human instinct. They may be elegant, beautiful, and so convincing that it's hard to imagine them being false – but concerning practical matters, no such thing is, in a final sense, objective. Even in science, concerning which great pains are taken to measure things accurately and repeatably, there is an important caveat to any and every theory: A theory is, and can only ever be, a model, a description of how things are *to us,* how things are *as measured by our instruments,* not necessarily what things numinously "really are." Science is precise, in the sense that we can have great confidence that theories corroborated by myriads of scientists will describe what we encounter in the future: but things that are not (or cannot be) tested in a rigorous science-like fashion cannot be treated with such a level of confidence. An ideology cannot be swallowed wholesale, a person cannot completely submerge themselves in the waters of an assumed truth, without drowning in fantasies, delusions, and lies.

Even if an actual *good* idea is adopted in an ideological way, simply accepted without thinking and asserted as absolutely true, serious problems could still arise. For one, a person will remain susceptible to the same phenomena that led them to accept this belief; these circumstances (such as emotional reactions to significant-seeming events, or even ordinary rhetoric) could lead a person to accept more destructive ideologies in other fields, or even to swap from their good idea to a worse, opposing idea, should the opposing idea hit them with a stronger emotional response. Another reason is that the person will lack the ability to convince another person of this good idea (having arrived at it through something other than careful reasoning), or even to defend their own beliefs if challenged. The realization of their inability to argue for this good idea might cause them to become frustrated, doubt it, and turn away from it despite its goodness. Therefore, if you think you have a good idea, you should make very sure that it actually stands up to serious questioning. How would a serious opponent, who is not merely trying to argue but sincerely trying to comprehend and critically think about your point of view, question you? How would they challenge the elements of your opinion which are not obvious to a layperson? Are you capable of responding to such questions?

The point of spelling all of this out, of giving these examples of emotional motivations behind opinions and ideologies, is not to say that all practical thought must be considered incorrect; merely that it is imperfect. The quintessential ideological trap is to assume that one has arrived at an unquestionable truth. Everything must be subject to questioning, everything must be tested and re-tested in order to make sure that it still stands. New ideas must be considered, even radical new ideas, wherever the old ideas seem to be inadequate, or seem to be beneath what we are capable of achieving – to do otherwise is to assume that the old ideas are unquestionable, infallible, perfect. Ideological beliefs are opinions, and no opinion is categorically superior to all others. All of these things are merely models, perspectives, abstractions of one's experiences, models which can never be perfect. One can only take these ideas, these elaborate amalgamations of many instinctual reactions, and try to put them to good use.

TRAINING WHEELS

As much evil as there is which can be laid at the feet of ideology, the fact remains that the principles of thought which lead to ideology are unavoidable, being an integral part of the human condition. Even ideology itself may be useful, in a certain sense, for a person's first attempts at modeling the world. In fact, something similar to ideology is always used as such – young people, people young enough that they literally do not have the education or life experience to understand the necessity for nuanced thought (let alone attain actual experience in developing nuanced patterns of thought), *cannot* think in anything but simplistic terms. Their thoughts are ideology-esque, oversimplified, overgeneralized, until both the need and the means to think in more nuanced terms appear, until something shocks them into realizing that a change in perspective is necessary.

This is one of the central reasons why it's important to be able to criticize one's own ideas. Yes, a person will assume by default that what they consider correct is correct, and yes, people will think in simple terms until the need for more nuance is presented to them as an urgent necessity; the fact that these things are the default behaviors of the human brain make it *all the more necessary* for any person, even someone who seems to be doing well in life, to subject their ideas to real criticism from time to time, to look for holes and errors and unresolved questions. These default behaviors can lead a person down an incorrect path – if they do not choose to look around from time to time and correct themselves. A person can go down such a path for a surprisingly long time before catching themselves – and some keep going down that very same path even *after* they catch themselves, burying their insecurities and doubts and simply continuing to go as they have gone before, simply because it is as they have gone before. It should not be an embarrassing thing to admit that you are wrong, but so many people so adamantly refuse to even consider it! There are probably readers at this very moment who are imagining to themselves, consciously or subconsciously, that the tendency towards ideology is something that they are immune to, and that these pages have been criticizing an entirely different class of person, a class which excludes them. Other readers are saying to themselves that they do subject their views to critical thought – but they are only *saying* this to themselves, trying to make themselves feel better, and in reality, they could not name a time when they admitted that they were wrong about any important topic in the past year. If you have the integrity to do so (that is, if you are above saying "I'm not smart enough," or worse, "I don't have the attention span"), take some time and make a mental exercise of challenging your own views; subject yourself to the hard questions, the scary questions, the ones that you don't like to go too deep into – go deep into them, and see what uncomfortable truths lie undiscovered. The truth is a powerful weapon once you are comfortable with it.

Ideology is a crude attempt to refine one's emotional inclinations into a rational formula, into a system of thought, into a manner of reasoning about the world. But even this, with all its potential for evil, is a step up from a complete lack of thinking. It is a way, a direction, a path – a path described by a crude map, but a map nonetheless. Again, for the person who is relatively naïve and only just learning to think about the future and contemplate the world, it is inevitable that something like ideology will manifest itself as their first semblance of a perspective; the key is to ensure that thought does not stop at this point. Ideology is an early sketch, which is better than a blank canvas, but an artist does not conclude their masterpiece at the stage of an early sketch. Ideology serves as the mental training wheels with which a person will gain their first inklings of how to navigate the world; but these training wheels must be discarded once it is obvious that they are no longer necessary, and are, in fact, a hindrance. Many people will cling to their training wheels, to that which brought them the ability to move in the first place, but this temptation must be overcome in order to make progress, to gain skills, and to move more freely. There are a few who would overtly say that they do not want more freedom, that they wish to keep their training wheels on; this is weakness, cowardice, and willful ignorance, all for the sake of a primitive sort of comfort within their status quo.

Tying this back in to the Question itself, the reader can hopefully see the progression, over the course of the first three parts of this book, of the various levels of acknowledgement and understanding of the Question: Outright refusal to address the Question, minimal acknowledgement of the Question via a trivial axiomatic answer, and the assumption of a simple answer, respectively. A person will probably find themselves proceeding through all three of these stages of comprehension in sequence before finding themselves capable of adequately addressing the Question. The final part of this book will describe the construction of a proper Answer.

PART IV: THE ANSWER

WHAT REMAINS?

An awful lot of human activity consists of the behaviors described in Parts I-III. All of these are inadequate methods of confronting the Question. Remove these things, and what remains? To arrive at an Answer, it is essential to eliminate everything unsatisfactory, to truly let go of the inadequate and insubstantial things that the world offers as distractions from the undeniable reality of the Question. Many things must be discarded, including things which many people consider to be quite important, and which people can and do make lengthy arguments about, in order to prove their importance. And to some people, these things may actually be truly important, these things may actually be a critical part of their Answer to the Question – but if they are not for you, you must discard them.

After the unnecessary things have been discarded, the remaining space must be searched for that which is what you want, that which is the best you can do, that which is so important that suicide can be forgotten (or at least postponed) until this search has yielded fruit. Active experimentation with an open but realistic mind, trying out all kinds of different activities, is one part of this search. To learn through experience a large number of different ways of living or potential directions in life will help to educate a person as to what they want. Your present idea of what you want may be uncertain, the direction toward what you want may be only vaguely known; but the more paths in life you try out, the more you will learn the difference between that which brings you closer and that which sends you further away; continue the process over time, and you will more and more accurately be able to measure your bearings. Camus framed this in terms of quantity over quality, the idea of deliberately undergoing a wide variety of life experiences as opposed to remaining reclusive until an opportunity for a "high-quality" activity appears. He also mentioned that quantity itself can influence quality, in the sense that a mass of a billion atoms differs in quality from a single atom. The practical experience to be gained from a large amount of experience in various areas of life will not only help to aid this search, but it will also be enjoyable for its own sake.

Another part of this search consists of purely intellectual efforts, deep introspection into what one considers truly valuable in life. This occurs in those moments of solitude that allow for the kind of reflection so often eclipsed by ordinary life activities – the big questions of existence. Who are you? Who do you want to be? What do you want to do? It's very easy to be so preoccupied with the demands and distractions of life that these moments of solitude go unnoticed, and very little time ends up being dedicated to truly *serious* thought about one's own life, mind, and self. It's entirely possible to live in a wretched, unhappy state for years and years, suffering all the while, without engaging in this sort of intellectual exercise, and to only retain a nebulous awareness that "something" is missing from one's life, without a clear idea of what exactly it could be. The exercise of deep thought, taking advantage of moments of solitude to contemplate one's position in a serious manner, may itself, as a life activity, be one of these missing pieces; performing it will certainly help anyone to find the rest of them. One method of inquiry you might use is a refined version of the "assuming the conclusion" tactic described in Part II. Even when it is not certain whether a question has an acceptable answer in the first place, it is reasonable to ask, "Supposing that there is a solution to this problem, what would a solution look like?" Even for the question of suicide, inquiries like this are perfectly reasonable ways of investigating the problem's solution space, so to speak. Suicide is a concrete thing, and so concrete questions can be asked about it. Some people may feel that it's improper, or even *disrespectful,* to try to subject the Question to critical thought. But when everything is on the line, every resource available ought to be used to make the most informed decision. Shutting out the reasoning parts of the mind, the parts which deal with long-term planning, leave only short-term whims and emotions in charge – a very risky strategy when death is on the table.

You will want to engage in every available method of searching in order to address the Question – and the more acute your awareness of the Question is, the more you will understand the urgency of progressing and refining this search. The ultimate target of this search is the best that you can possibly do, that which you want most to achieve with your life, that which will improve the world to the highest degree that you can manage. This is the search for what you want.

BEING SELF-CRITICAL

When evaluating the big questions, one of the most important principles is to acknowledge is that you could be wrong. This is deceptively difficult to do properly – many readers are undoubtedly saying to themselves at this very moment, "Yes, I'm able to acknowledge that I could be wrong. I'm not some dumb barbarian or delusional narcissist. The things that I believe in are the product of all my years of experience, analyzed through my own critical thought process, and they are subject to further criticism." But in spite of how nice it might sound to say something so self-congratulatory, what if you're still completely and utterly wrong about something important? What would it take for you to acknowledge it?

It's easy to criticize other people for swallowing such-and-such ideological belief, but again, it's hard to properly criticize yourself along the same lines – or at least, to *start* criticizing yourself, to make this critical change in your mindset, in your perception of the world. Some people think they're already doing it, when they're not. Other people literally don't care, and just do what they've always been doing, think how they've always thought, simply "gotten by" with whatever method they think "works" for them (even if all the evidence indicates that it's actually working very poorly for them).

Here's a useful thought experiment, which I call "The Straight-Face Test." The reader, especially the young reader, is encouraged to apply this test to any belief they have that seems to be the subject of frequent dispute or controversy, no matter how certain the reader is of its validity or how popular (or unpopular) it is. The test is as follows: Imagine explaining such-and-such belief to a reasonably open-minded stranger, who does not agree with your claim, but is willing to hear you out, no matter how extreme or unusual your case may be (or appear to them). Imagine how this situation would actually play out, in real life. Can you deliver a thorough explanation of your beliefs with a straight face? This means several things – First, can you convey this information at all without feeling embarrassed, without feeling like you don't really know what you're talking about? If not, you probably don't believe in this thing as strongly as you think you do, possibly because you don't really understand it. If you don't understand something, saying you believe in it is a lie. Second, can you explain this set of beliefs from the ground up, in your own terms, without resorting to quoting someone else? If not, you might have been taken in by someone else's rhetoric, rather than actually being convinced of the belief itself. Third, can you explain the bottom line of your beliefs? Can you explain "what should be done about it," or better yet, "what *you* intend to do about it"? These need to be concrete things – it doesn't count if it's simply your hobby to "research it" or "spread the word about it." If you can't connect this belief of yours with substantial action, you might only be humoring this "belief" as a means of entertainment, because you think it's funny or cool. Or worse, you might only have adopted this "belief" out of desperation to pigeonhole yourself, to be part of a group, to have a "something" to make into part of your "identity." Fourth, after you have made your explanation and this person starts to question and criticize your claims – and this will absolutely happen in practice – how do you expect the conversation to go? Don't think about what you would like to do, or what you think would be best to do; think about *how you would actually react in this kind of social situation.* If, for example, you would likely feel an urge to start speaking very quickly, to get as many of your points into the conversation as possible as quickly as possible, that may mean your belief isn't very sincere – yes, even if you yourself consider it to be a sincere belief. If you feel this sort of panic as a reaction to your ideas being questioned, it means you aren't very confident in your ability to argue for this thing, and that you probably don't know what you're talking about, as much as you'd like to think you do. Consider how the conversation would go, take the perspective of a very skeptical person; imagine how someone intelligent and reasonable would criticize your beliefs, and see how easy (or difficult) it is to defend them. If you find a belief extraordinarily difficult to defend, perhaps the belief is wrong. Importantly, throughout this thought experiment, you must be sure to use terms and assumptions in your defense that *even a person whose beliefs are contrary to yours* would understand and accept. It wouldn't make much sense to require that a person must be already be convinced of your beliefs in order to be convinced of them.

The general theme in the above test is that if you cannot explain your beliefs thoroughly, then either you do not believe in them in general, or you have not thought about them very thoroughly, and in particular, not very *critically*. If you find that one or more of your key beliefs fails this test, don't worry. If you can understand and accept this, then you will have grown as a person, you will have grown out of a bogus ideological stint.

ORIGINS OF DESIRES

It has been repeated throughout this book that you cannot assume that any of your ideas are absolutely correct. Let's look more carefully into why this is. As explained in the "Rational" subsection of Part III, you are an animal, and your ideas, the things which you call rational thoughts, are aggregated responses to a large number of situations – you might think of a complex thought as an amalgamation of many smaller desires, each one reflecting the desired outcome of some individual past situation that you experienced. Others, the genetically-induced instincts of the body, have been bred into us by eons of evolution, automatic responses adapted to the common experiences of our countless ancestors. The ability of the brain to interpret such a wide range of experiences in concert, to track the multifaceted patterns between them and to make predictions and judgments based on many of them simultaneously, is what makes the human mind so powerful. At the bottom of your motivations lie an intricate symphony of primitive desires.

As highly as the human brain might think of itself, the fact is that it is finite. The elaborate models that it forms can be, and often are, grossly flawed. Even the least-attentive person is aware that people are often wrong, even when they think they're right – that is, even when their mental model, which they have constructed and refined with years of life experience, says that they're right. Everyone knows that people can be wrong; what should be acknowledged more often is that the set of people who can be wrong includes *you*. The illustration of thoughts as being an intricate combination of simple, rudimentary desires is meant to remind the reader that a thought about any topical issue, however confident you may be in it, cannot be considered "simply right" in the sense that one plus one equals two is "simply right." Definitive truths like a triangle having three sides, or elementary logical rules such as De Morgan's laws, are totally unambiguous – these kinds of propositions, these "relations between ideas" as Hume describes them, can be evaluated as true or false with a certainty that propositions about practical matters simply cannot. To consider one's position on, say, immigration policy, to be equally unambiguously correct is nonsense. But that's just it: because it's easier to think one-dimensionally, people do assume such simple things, that something is "simply right" or "simply wrong," more often than not. A person will default to thinking in simple terms rather than nuanced terms until a need to account for more detail is made clear – to them personally, in circumstances that they personally will respond to.

The fact of human thought being composed of rudimentary desires is not a bad thing. Some may try to present a misanthropic or antinatalist perspective using this fact as an excuse, but such arguments don't really hold any water. Would you consider a concerto worthless because someone described it as a collection of individual sounds? Of course not. The whole argument is ultimately just an appeal to the aesthetic claim of the primitive or animalistic being bad, which is a rather ignorant claim in the first place – not to mention a self-defeating one. Does the thought of being motivated by such shallow things as emotions fill you with negative emotion?

Even one's highest and most noble goals come from these humble origins, which leads to the interesting consequence that great deeds (both good and evil) might be performed for very simple reasons. Perhaps a person finds it difficult to sleep, or finds that food tastes poor, or finds little pleasure in relaxation, or otherwise seems to be hindered from being happy – whenever they neglect to do the things that they consider best and most important, whenever they fail to do what they want. Perhaps a person notices that they only feel truly happy and satisfied when they are being (what they consider to be) a good person, and so they act as (what they consider to be) a good person: partially because they consider it "good" on an intellectual level, and partially because it feels "good" on a more corporeal level. The bodily "feeling good" aspect of this is also not a problem. This only means that you have a functioning conscience, and your rational mind is in agreement with the rest of you. There might be some who would claim that doing good things because it feels good to do so is somehow illegitimate and not "truly" good, inasmuch as the sensory "feeling good" is perceived as a reward – but what's the alternative, exactly? Conditioning yourself somehow such that you feel bad when doing good things, and then doing good things anyway? This would just be the same outcome plus unnecessary suffering. Like the antinatalist argument mentioned above, that kind of claim is just a play on the notion that something primitive, like sensation as the means of reward and punishment, is automatically bad.

To be fair, in practice, it is entirely possible to rely too much on individual incidents of sensing pain and pleasure, punishment and reward on a microscopic scale, and to neglect to use one's intellect to make more comprehensive judgments. Being hasty in such judgments can lead to prejudice and other behaviors described in Part III. Failing to make such judgments entirely can lead a person to wind up woefully unprepared for the future as a whole, and other consequences described in Part II. In the extreme case, a person might develop a sort of naïve hedonism, being totally unmotivated to do anything that does not promise instant gratification; it would easy for a person in a condition like this to turn to drug or food addiction, gambling, or chronic obsession with sex or pornography. A person may, due to some coincidence, ascribe the wrong causes to their feelings of punishment and reward, and wind up seeking out things that they do not really want, and avoiding things that they do not really want to avoid. This can lead to the difficult situation where a person acts as if they want something, or as if they want to avoid something, not because it's actually what they want to do, but simply because they've done it so many times. A newly adopted dog barks at a person it's never met before; if it sees this person every day for years without incident, the dog may still bark at them, not because it has any reason to be afraid, but simply because it has become a habit, because barking at that person is "the thing to do." All habits, especially those that take up a lot of time or effort, or which may seem troublesome or weird to people (including yourself), should be subject to careful inspection. Traditions are habits that cross generations; the principle applies to these as well.

What you want, whatever it is, will also have its origins in primitive, simple desires, because it will be, in essence, a collection of human thoughts. Do not be ashamed of these humble origins, do not despise yourself for being an animal. Do the things you want, do not be ashamed of your happiness, even if it is superficial; do not be the stereotypical teenager who, desperate to become their ideal image of a sophisticated adult, takes everything far too seriously, becoming humorless. Do what you want, and be proud of yourself when you have done it, and allow yourself to relish the happiness of your pride. Meanwhile, equally importantly, do not be so pretentious as to imagine that the conclusions your finite nervous system has developed are anything remotely comparable to the absolute, objective, or infallible. And for the same reasons, as explained in Part III, do not assume that what any other human being, or collection of human beings, has produced is absolutely true either. What our species has made over time are many models of many things, and some are better than others, and some will last longer than others, and some could conceivably last forever. In the overwhelming majority of cases, though, absolute certainty is beyond the scope of human comprehension; anyone who says otherwise is selling something.

SKEPTICISM

Hopefully, readers who have gotten this far have already understood that a book is something to read, not to swallow; and that includes this book. I do not want readers to go through this book with the impression that I am declaring infallible, unquestionable truth here. I would be a hypocrite to say such a thing – all I can say is that I believe in what is written here. One of the central messages of this book is thinking for yourself, as opposed to merely swallowing the words of others because they sound nice or they come from some respected authority. So do not imagine that this book is something unquestionable; put it to the test, as a sensible, reasonable, critically-thinking person would. Are its propositions true? Are its recommendations useful? I think that they are – but if you find that some of them are not, do not cling to them just because others in the same book are useful. And vice versa: do not reject anything useful simply because it occurs in the same book as something useless. This is an area where it's very easy to think in too-simple terms, to think one-dimensionally; do not act as if everything in the world must be either completely good or completely bad, infallibly useful or unsalvageably useless. Just as a person can do both good and evil in one lifetime, a book (or any other collection of information) can contain both good and bad material. Use what is good, let go of what is bad, and be careful not to develop biases based on associations that aren't actually relevant.

Further, I challenge readers to apply this same standard to every other source of information they receive, every book they read, everything they hear on TV, on the Internet, and in normal conversation. This is ordinary skepticism – it's not a difficult standard to employ, though it may be unfamiliar in certain contexts to certain readers. Do not be quick to swallow something just because it appears attractive for whatever reason; do not be quick to block something out of your consciousness entirely just because it appears ugly for whatever reason. Use your head, think for yourself, don't just cling to the first emotional reaction that is instantaneously brought on by, say, a news story or a social media headline.

To more tangibly illustrate the necessity for this skeptical attitude, go to some online forum where it's possible to make anonymous comments, comments not tied to your real person; the more anonymity and the less strict moderation, the better. Immerse yourself in the online environment and see what it's like to treat it as a source of information. People will spout claim after claim; check these claims, *both the ones you would like to believe and the ones you wouldn't,* for yourself. Do a little online research, see in each case if what they're saying is actually verifiable or whether they're just pulling it out of their proverbial ass. If someone were to tell you, as a piece of advice, "People can and often do lie on the Internet," you will most likely agree, and indeed, consider it as so obvious as to go without saying – but some people tend to forget this key fact in-the-moment when consuming information online. A little practice in this exercise will reveal to you just how unreliable people's statements can be – but nonetheless, how tempting it is, on certain occasions, to simply believe what you see by default, without scrutiny!

After that, observe more carefully-curated and strictly-moderated websites and other information sources, and repeat the same exercise. Though certain kinds of blatantly-inaccurate information might be cut down somewhat, the same fundamental lack of trustworthiness remains in these places too. In particular, when you see someone make a claim about a topic or event that you haven't studied in-depth, part of you might be tempted to accept it by default, to think to yourself something like this: "Well, if this person is simply lying then the statement wouldn't be here, it would have been removed or censored somehow! It must have been fact-checked by someone. Or, at the very least, it can't be something patently false, because if it was, the person who made this statement would know it could be easily proven false, and so he wouldn't have wasted his own time by telling such an easily-disprovable lie. So it must be true." But this is far too optimistic, far too trusting, especially if the claim is from a complete stranger. When you see a statement like that, stop yourself before you accept it wholesale, and look into the facts yourself. Why do you think so many social media websites have been emphasizing their efforts to combat misinformation? Because it's a huge, pervasive phenomenon, in spite of all the protective measures already in place.

Be skeptical towards all information that comes your way – and be *especially* wary of anyone who has money or other material gain to be made by either convincing people of a claim, attracting people to view an information source (such as a website or TV channel), or simply publicly making a claim in the first place. Granted, not everybody who's in it for the money is a liar, but it's extremely easy to become a liar when you're in it for the money. Imagine a fresh college graduate who's just been hired by a major news organization, and they're tasked to write a story for publication in a certain way; the new hire observes that the desired product would be either omitting critical information, biased so heavily as to be unethical, or an outright lie to the audience. If the new hire goes to their supervisor and objects, they'll be told something like: "it's your job, and if you don't want to do it, there's the door." If they are not treated even more harshly, that is. A lot of people are in it for the money out of necessity; for how many of these people is journalistic integrity more important than a paycheck, i.e., survival above the level of poverty? And for those who actually would quit under such circumstances, how many other candidate hires are waiting, who would concede to whatever unscrupulous task is given to them? The fact of the latter's existence would likely hinder many (typically) morally upstanding individuals from quitting in the first place. And this is all not even mentioning those who are "in it for the money" in a more nefarious sense. Yes, anyone who is selling you some kind of information for a living (including situations where the customer receives the information for free while the producer makes money off of advertising) should be viewed with the utmost scrutiny. And on the Internet in particular, native advertising has emerged as a new tactic – anyone on the web that you don't know could be a potential salesman. Keep the ancient wisdom in mind: "Don't believe everything you see on the Internet."

LETTING GO

Once again, the temptation to cling to ideology and other such simplistic manners of thinking is extremely strong, and a person will find it extremely difficult even to diagnose the issue in themselves, let alone let go of it. But there are ways to do it, to admit it, and to let go.

First, the big obstacle: admitting that you have a problem, that there is *something* about your manner of thinking that you could improve. Naturally, your base assumption, your null hypothesis so to speak, is that you are correct, and you will maintain this hypothesis until proven otherwise – but you should admit that it *can* be proven otherwise. You are human, you can be wrong. It will be useful to recall and admit to yourself, as evidence of this, occasions where you made a claim without really knowing what you were talking about, or other such occasions evidenced in *actual, real-life events*; this will help you to understand tangibly that there are still flaws in your mind, that your reasoning is not perfect; and this is okay. But if you want to become more perfect in actuality, you will need to make some actual changes to the way you think.

Once the possibility of harboring incorrect or troublesome thoughts is understood, the next task is to push and pull and pick and prod at your own thoughts. Carefully sift through and test the ideas that motivate what you think and what you do, and find those ideas which cannot stand up to real criticism – and then, if it's certain that they do not help you, but only hinder you, remove them. Let go of them. Some people, who feel a strong sensation of offense and betrayal when they find that one of their ideas is unworthy of this clinging, may be tempted to instantly jump and cling to the opposite of the abandoned idea; but this is disadvantageous for obvious reasons. It is best not to cling to ideas at all if you can avoid it.

It would also be easy at any point to stop the thought experiment short, to stop caring, and to continue with life as usual – but to improve requires effort. There will likely be parts of you that desperately want to cling to your deep-seated ideas, even after noticing that they don't really stand up to close scrutiny. A person who is inclined towards some sort of prejudice, for example, might be quick to say to themselves, "Even so, I refuse to believe it! How can *those people* be any good whatsoever? Just look at them! Just look at what they're doing!" Perhaps there is some image you have in your head that you consider intimately tied to this type of person, some stereotype of appearance or action, and you find it hard to imagine *those people*, whoever they might be, without thinking of some kind of repulsive image. In that case, there are two important possibilities you will want to examine: either that the image is not actually as strongly correlated with *those people* as you think; or that the image is only repulsive in image, and not actually representative of some kind of serious moral wrong. Your actual opinions might be more tolerant than you realize – yes, even if you've got the kind of personality that is attracted to intolerance, the kind that finds it fun to fantasize about superiority. Once again, for emphasis: *it is okay to change your mind.*

And prejudice is only one example. Any kind of immediately emotionally-motivated thought should be subject to the same kind of criticism. Here is the red flag to look out for, as you look at your own thoughts: when a particular topic comes up, or when you are contradicted somehow regarding this topic, how quickly do you become angry, or fearful? The more immediate it is, the more the opinion should be doubted. If a person says something really outlandish like "actually, serial killers are good for society" and seems to be serious about it, the normal response isn't anger or fear, but bewilderment. Anger and fear as a response to political or social discourse should always be checked. The improvements to ordinary conversation that come from having a more robust opinion are obvious; and there are additional practical benefits. Say that some person, some celebrity or wannabe celebrity, does something stupid in a very public and extremely provocative manner. If you feel angry as a result, and you post your opinion about this person and this incident on the Internet, *you've just given this person free advertising.* Publicity stunts of all sorts hinge on people reacting with anger or fear, stirring up manufactured controversy, because that makes people repeat the name of the relevant person or product or event in public forums. And that's advertising. Do you think that marketing professionals don't know this? Do you think they haven't considered this as a potential avenue for spreading the word for their product? For some people, it may even be their *primary* method of gaining attention. If you don't want to be someone else's unpaid salesman, a good first step is to insulate yourself from being offended by such things, and especially acting out this offense in public forums. You will also become less vulnerable to people trying to sell you things you don't need, or trying to coerce you into a lifestyle that won't actually bring you what you want.

The axiomatic position against suicide from Part II should be subjected to this level of scrutiny as well. Is this inclination toward life motivated by emotion, rather than reason? Is it based on an instinctive reaction rather than a careful judgment of possibilities, benefits, costs? The fundamental problems with this have already been discussed, but there is also an auxiliary problem: if the position of being against suicide (a most important topic) is formed based on spur-of-the-moment emotions, a person may feel, consciously or subconsciously, that it is okay to form other opinions in other fields based on similarly unstable reasoning. Granted, in both the case of suicide and the general case, it may be that your gut feeling is correct – but it is best not to take the risk, best not to immediately assume correctness and cease all further thought. It is best to be able to prove that your convictions are legitimate, to be able to prove it to yourself and to others.

"YOU HAVE TO"

The unqualified "you have to" is restriction in its purest and least justified form. Every ideological precept described in Part III is a "you have to" – you have to believe this, you have to do that, you have to speak like this, you have to act like that, you have to imagine the world as such-and-such. The central flaw of ideology is its restrictive nature, and the unqualified phrase "you have to" is restriction solely for the sake of restriction. In *Thus Spoke Zarathustra,* Nietzsche refers to a golden dragon with "Thou shalt" written on every scale, which declares: "All values have already been created, and all created values – are in me. Truly, there shall be no more 'I will!'"

The phrase "you have to," in order to have meaning, requires a qualification. "You have to have a job in order to make money." "You have to go to school if you want to get such-and-such kind of job." "You have to obey traffic laws if you want to keep yourself and others safe." This is how information is conveyed. This is obvious; the real trouble, the very subtle and sneaky trouble, is in the "you have to" that you quietly, but no less insistently, tell yourself.

To live your life according to a code of what you think you "have to" do is dangerous. In your mind, when you think of why you intend to do such-and-such thing, an unqualified mental answer of "because I have to," being a simple and easy and one-dimensional answer, is likely to occur to a lot of people, without their grasping the depth of what this kind of answer implies. If there is no deeper thought than the phrase "I have to," if the reasons behind an action are not truly explored, but only insisted upon, perhaps clung to out of habit or fear, hidden dangers grow and fester. One danger is that the idea itself may be a bad idea, something self-destructive, destructive to others, or a useless waste of time, or something blindly carried out under the orders of some other person, or some false impression. The other danger is that the idea itself is actually a good idea – *but the conceptualization of it as something you "have to" do can make it seem like the opposite.* If you "have to" do something, there is no question about it, no choice to be made. If you tell yourself that you "have to" do something, you are telling yourself that you have already been coerced, restricted, forced into it, with no other option available. If you have been imprisoned in this way, if your actions have been restricted in this way, is it not natural to try to escape? Couldn't even a very good idea, once obeyed under the childlike mantra of "I have to do it, so I'll do it," come to seem like an adversary and a tyrannical restriction?

It is an essential step in addressing the Question to understand the real extent of your freedom, your freedom to choose in spite of the impressions that you have received from other people, in spite of the expectations that other people seem to have, in spite of what is "normal," and in spite of the ideal images of your future self that you may have once built up under those influences. To truly weigh your options, as will occur in the course of determining the answers to deep existential questions, you must look at them through the widest possible lens, to see as much as possible, to let nothing be restricted from your view. Yes, there are things that almost everybody wants to do; almost everybody wants to be healthy, to pursue happiness, to contribute to the world somehow, to have enjoyable and useful relationships with other people, and so on. But none of these things, strictly speaking, are things that you "have to" do.

The unqualified "you have to" reveals itself as nonsense when subject to examination. For example, you do not have to go to college; there are many jobs that you can get which do not require a college degree. You do not have to get a normal job; there are other ways of making money. You do not have to make money; there are methods of living which will allow you to survive without it. Lastly, you do not have to survive; life is not a condition which is forced upon you, once you have both an awareness of the concept of suicide and the ability to perform it.

AN OPTION

Finally, we arrive at the heart of it all: the importance of acknowledging suicide as an option. It is a fact that a person can commit suicide. It is physically possible. It is an option. As explained in Parts I and II, the rejection of this fact is a denial of reality, complete with all the problems that will inevitably spring from any denial of reality. The belief that one has no such option, that life is forced upon a person, is a denial of reality, and, ironically enough, it will breed unnecessarily negative attitudes towards life.

A person tells themselves that they have been imprisoned in the world of the living. Will the part of them that loves freedom not seek to escape from this prison? Will this not be a constant irritation, an itch in the back of the mind, that a state of imprisonment is something to escape from? Will it not remain there and grow and grow in the subconscious (once it has existed for a long time without contradiction), while the flawed notion that one "has to" keep living shrinks away? In the eventual moment of crisis, how great will be the desire to escape in comparison to the presupposition of "I have to," the mantra of "I have to keep living"? Which of the two will be more powerful?

You cannot choose between life and death if you fail to acknowledge that a choice exists. You cannot answer the question of suicide if you fail to see that there is, in fact, a question – that is, with more than one conceivable answer. The fact is that life is voluntary. "I want to" sounds far better than "I have to;" would you rather say "I want to live" or "I have to live"? The decision to either live or die is in your hands; to address the resulting Question adequately, you must cast aside all illusions of "I have to" and see the freedom inherent in life as it is – up to and including the freedom to bring your own life to an end. If every element of your life was motivated not by an "I have to," but instead by an "I want to," what would the resulting life look like? Would it look good enough that suicide can be set aside, perhaps even forgotten? With the greatest possible set of options before you, with absolutely everything physically possible to you also on the table, death is on the table – and it is a fact that you will reach your death at some point. But is there anything else that you may be interested in, that you wish to see before the end?

ANOTHER OPTION

An equally important option to acknowledge is that of slow suicide, continuing to live but doing absolutely nothing, culminating in the death of an already-forgotten nobody. In the grand scheme of things, a person who commits suicide while young and a person who simply does nothing for a few more decades before incidentally dying are identical – nothing is accomplished between youth and death, whether the period in between is a matter of days or years. It is possible to commit suicide by old age.

Once again: this is an option. It is in the realm of the possible for you (yes, even you!) to do this. In fact, suicide by old age is probably one of the most common ways that a person's life ends nowadays. If you do not do what you want, if you do not make a conscious effort to play seriously at this game of life, this is the fate that awaits you by default. In today's society, a person can do very little and still survive for a long time. Will you take advantage of the assumption that you will easily be able to remain alive in the future, without having to do anything, and will you gamble on the hope that, during this time, something will compel you to do the things that you want in life?

How many people live their lives exactly like this, I wonder? How many people go through life, failing to act again and again, telling themselves every day that they will start doing what they want tomorrow, or next week, or next year, but never reaching *today*? It is possible, even common, to fail at life, to have no hopes and no prospects, to have a long history of not doing what you want, and no real plans to change this. Because this unthinking and uncaring lifestyle is the default, that which requires the minimal effort to sustain, it is probably more common, more *likely,* than you realize – even for you. Now, some readers may be tempted to point to all of their friends and family, who all seem to have bright futures ahead, and imagine that this is an exaggeration, to say to themselves, "What do you mean, live a whole life doing nothing? Everyone I know is doing all kinds of great things in life!" But if you, dear reader, are a college graduate with what a college graduate would call "a decent job," I would like to remind you that you are not a normal person. You have already brought yourself above "normal" in at least one important way. Normal people are the people you see on the bus, at the DMV, in hospital waiting rooms, at the county fair. If you have ever worked as a cashier in a budget-friendly retail store or a fast-food restaurant, the customers you served were largely normal people. Normal people are what crowds are made of. Normal people are the ones who consistently buy things that are heavily advertised – and they cause these things, regardless of their actual quality, to become the most popular. The average adult in the United States is overweight, bordering on obese, and has an Associate's Degree at best, if they went to college at all.

This is what it means to be normal. Knowing how common these things are, perhaps it's easier to understand how common it is, how *easy* it is, to live a life of absolutely no significance. And because you are a human being, it is an option for you too. Aspire, then, to be greater than normal.

PURPOSE

Imagine a person who has no answer, not even a secret answer that they keep hidden within their heart, to the question "Why have you not yet ended yourself?" Imagine a person who has not even slightly considered their potential impact upon the world, or any kind of purpose that they might develop in life. Imagine a person who wakes up, eats food, drinks water, breathes air, sleeps, works, acquires and spends money, all without having a purpose in doing so. Imagine a person who could not speak in defense of their own existence – *even if their existence itself was at stake.* It is a grim fact that such people exist, and many of them will never construct answers to such questions, such challenges.

In the workplace, when funding is distributed for new projects, at some point, everything will have to be defended in front of a stakeholder. Some very important person, someone whose decision will determine whether the project will receive funding or be put on the chopping block, will need to be swayed by this defense. While any number of colorful graphics and name-drops of trendy technologies might glamorize the presentation, the bottom line will remain in the stakeholder's mind: What is this all for? What's the point? What am I funding this for? There are three ways this can be answered: a straightforward and truthful answer, a successful lie, or a failed lie. A failed lie will result in the project being discarded without a second thought. A successful lie will cause the program to receive funding, but it will hang by a thread; if any previous lie is uncovered, or if any subsequent lie is detected, then the program will either have its funding cut, or it will continue to no benefit and to a massive waste of money; and either way, someone involved in that lie will get in very serious trouble. As stakeholders are always highly scrutinizing about what they spend their money on, a "successful" lie will never be successful for long. A truthful defense of the project is, of course, the best option; even if the project is rejected, it will prove a learning experience to all parties involved, and a significant amount of unnecessary trouble will be avoided compared to the other two options.

In the above metaphor, the project is the individual's life, and the individual is both the presenter and the stakeholder. When someone cannot defend *even to themselves* the purpose of their own life, danger is imminent. Any lie told to oneself, any distraction meant to entertain oneself and avoid difficult questions altogether, is certain to fail in the end. Unlike the rare occasion of a high-stakes business meeting, the interactions between the behaviors of the self and the perception of the self occur constantly. While consciousness of such interactions can be muffled by distractions, this consciousness will never cease entirely. The self cannot be fooled forever. There will arise a point in time, in some deep loneliness, where no distraction is possible and the questions of one's own existence cannot be avoided. These critical questions, which must be answered in order to evaluate one's life as successful or unsuccessful on a fundamental level, will at some point reveal themselves. Those who do not wish to see such experiences as crushing or humiliating, those who would rather experience such things with something like pride, are well encouraged to meditate upon the deep questions as frequently as possible, and to work as hard as possible to develop meaningful answers to them. What sort of life are you funding, exactly, with this money that you make at your job? For what purpose are you eating this food, breathing this air? What, in your old age, would you like to say you have achieved? What impact will you have on this world? What are the continuing effects that your life will have produced, after your death?

Again, those who have failed to some degree in their lives will feel pressured to avoid acknowledging the question entirely. The most susceptible to this pressure are the type who prefer to allow problems to occur, and suffer the pain of the consequences (either pretending it's "unavoidable" or "out of nowhere," or else ignoring it), rather than take the less painful options that would prevent their problems in the first place. The avoidant "strategy" is a sure route to failure. Failing to address existential questions will cause a person's existence to fail in the long term. In the purposeless individuals who neglect such things, there may arise a sort of desperation, an urgent desire to seek out "something new, something new," all the time, some new distraction, it doesn't matter what sort, anything to avoid the horror of one's own failures made apparent by ordinary self-reflection. Imagine being such a failure that the prospect of reflecting on your own life, on a basic level, frightens you. It would be best to see nobody fall to such a state; but concerning those who do anyway, the worst thing is to continue the lie. It is far better to confront the truth, make a genuine recovery, and grow as a person. Is this not common knowledge? Is any of this surprising?

WORTHLESS DEATH

Death is inevitable; trying to avoid it altogether is folly. The object to be avoided is not death itself, but the premature death, the worthless death, the death that cements the life that preceded it as a worthless life. This includes, of course, death in either young or old age. As explained earlier, a person can live a worthless life for 60, 70, 80 years. It's easy in today's world to live for a long time without doing anything. Even making a large number of serious mistakes will often not kill you, but rather, you will find yourself continuing to live for a long time, even in a very damaged or degraded condition.

The worthless death at old age is to be avoided; to avoid it is to do what you want before you become too old to be physically or mentally capable of it. The worthless death at young age is to be avoided; to avoid it is to postpone suicide (of the unwarranted type) and minimize reckless behavior, such as drunk driving and taking drugs from strangers (as opposed to bold, decisive action in general, which some small-minded people will call "reckless" simply because it goes against the grain or seems frightening or sudden). There is also the ever-present possibility of accidental death. You could be hit by a reckless driver, struck by lightning, or involved in some other freak accident at any time. However unlikely it may be at any given moment, if you keep on postponing what you want, the odds become less and less remote that you will be killed or maimed in an accident at some point in between the present and your moment of action. The same goes for disease and senescence. Will you wait until you are old and crippled before doing what you want? If, on that day, you find yourself unable to, will you simply shrug and say that you must have been destined never to achieve anything?

In much the same way, it is not suicide itself which is to be avoided, but the pointless suicide, the suicide that concludes a life that never achieved anything, the suicide that serves no benefit but only destroys. This includes suicide by old age, but excludes such things as martyrdom. For the young reader, and even for middle-aged readers, the time between the present and death is wide and open. Easy though it might be to make excuses, to say "it's too late for me," is every culture in the world not teeming with true stories of people who successfully transformed their lives from unbearably bad to prodigiously good? Will you simply brush off the existence of such people, considering yourself to be in an entirely different class from them, in spite of the fact that you would become such a person yourself if you did the very thing which lies in front of you, the very thing that you *most want to do?*

JUST...

It is only by reaching this point, the point of serious contemplation of suicide, that you can really recognize the magnitude of your freedom, the freedom to *do what you want.* It is only when death itself has truly been weighed as an option, it is only when even the survival instinct itself has been called into question and made into a secondary priority, secondary to *what you want,* that the truth reveals itself. If the question of your very existence is subject to *what you want,* then so is everything else. Every "you have to" is on the chopping block, every thou-shalt and thou-shalt-not is up for debate. Every idea, however concrete, can potentially be pruned away – once it is acknowledged that life itself can be pruned away.

Discarding the kind of unnecessary beliefs described in Part III can be difficult if a person has not really weighed the Question in all its seriousness. Ideological beliefs can be instilled as firmly as the survival instinct itself; sometimes people even tell the truth when they say they would die for what they believe. A person can consider such beliefs to be utterly intrinsic to their character, and betrayal of these beliefs as unthinkable as suicide. Now, maybe some of these beliefs are actually legitimate, actually worth believing in and worth dying for – but then again, maybe not. And if no argument or evidence from an outside party can convince a person to question such beliefs, is there anything that could? What would be enough to convince such an obstinate person to change their mind? It would have to be something from within their own mind – the Question, which looms unavoidably in every person's thought, is that final catalyst which is able to spur the reevaluation (or, perhaps, the first serious evaluation) of one's fundamental beliefs.

This huge and terrible catharsis, this throwing of all preconceived value-judgments into chaos and uncertainty, is necessary for a person to adopt a critical mindset at the deepest level. This is why every mature person has considered suicide: it is necessary to consider it seriously, critically, honestly, in a truly *open-*

minded sense, and to weigh every possibility concerning it; otherwise, you don't even know whether you want to exist in the first place. And if someone doesn't really know such a basic thing as that, do they really know anything? Who would trust their judgment? Would they even trust themselves? If such a person were to realize that they don't trust themselves, it would be in their interest to get to the root of the problem – and to start as quickly as possible.

The person who contemplates suicide is full of doubt; this is advantageous. Doubt is the weapon by which the tyrants of the mind are overthrown. "A single man who stops lying can bring down a tyranny." To stop lying, you must be honest; to be honest, you must think critically; to think critically, you must doubt. Therefore, to stop lying to yourself about life, you must first doubt life, and once this is done, the chains of the mind can be broken. Every ideological knot in your brain can be untied; every ideological cage that you have locked yourself into can be unlocked; it's just that a person must be willing to *doubt* on a high level, in order to realize that their "beliefs" are incoherent, tangled-up knots, and that their "way of life" is a cramped, uncomfortable cage. And how many new and exciting possibilities open themselves once this is done! Expressing your opinion becomes as simple as speaking your mind, the words naturally flowing out – it no longer requires navigating a tangled-up maze of fixed ideas that "have to" be considered true, with which everything "has to" align. Pursuing your goals becomes as simple as *doing what you want,* the actions coming naturally to mind and seeming so easy, simply because they are what you want – it no longer requires a neurotic scrambling to ensure that every action is in alignment with the thou-shalts and thou-shalt-nots commanded by one's religion, culture, parents, peer pressure, or any other such thing. All unnecessary biases, whether towards superficial things like pleasure, or more complex things like the demands of other people – everything is subsidiary to what you want.

Let your mantra be *"I do what I want."* Let your overarching commandment, to which everything else (up to and including your own survival) is subsidiary, be *"Do what you want."* Just do what you want. Doesn't the phrase have a nice ring to it? From this fundamental principle, everything proceeds.

OBJECTION

Undoubtedly, some readers will recoil when they read the words "do what you want." How many people throughout all ages have used this phrase as a half-baked mantra, an excuse to stop thinking and act haphazardly, rather than recognizing the concept's true potential! If it isn't obvious, that phrase is used here in its strictest sense: do what you *really* want, what you *truly* want, what you honestly believe will bring you towards a life that does not deserve to be destroyed prematurely. The things that you want, in the proper sense, are the things that are important enough that death can be postponed until they are achieved. Even after making this clear, though, some readers will still hesitate to accept the use of this phrase. To some readers, doing what you want is a dangerous, alien concept; the instinctive tendency to recoil from the dangerous and alien can be hard to suppress.

For example, a reader might object: "What if what I want to do is just sit around and watch TV all day, and do nothing?" To this, I would respond: Well, do you? Do you actually consider that to be what you truly want out of life? The very fact of raising it as an objection suggests that you consider it something undesirable, something which you are not confident in. On the other hand, it's not impossible to transform a desire of that kind into something more meaningful, something which a person could comfortably say *is* what they want out of life; some people could satisfy a desire of this sort and simultaneously do some kind of important work, for example, by becoming a film critic. Or, less intensively, it could be incorporated as a smaller part what a person wants; someone could simply watch TV or movies or play video games as a hobby, to rest in between some other work which is more important to them. A discerning person would also develop taste in these media, expressing their individual preferences, thus making their hobbies into something more than mere distraction, but rather, an expression of their personality, more strongly a part of what they want.

Again, a reader might object: "What if I want to kill people? Should I simply give in to that desire?" I offer the same response: Do you? If you actually feel a strong desire to do such things, you should probably consider seeing a psychologist, because thoughts of that type are not normal and are considered very dangerous. And again, a person might be able to sublimate this desire into something less destructive and more useful: maybe what such a person really wants is not to kill, but to fight, to demonstrate physical strength; such a person might become a martial arts expert, a professional fighter, or some kind of instructor in a similar field.

Here is another important detail to bear in mind: to properly want something is to want both the thing itself and everything that it entails. To want to eat copious amounts of unhealthy food and live a sedentary lifestyle is to want to become fat and unhealthy. You can't truly want the thing without wanting the consequences; if you don't want the consequences, you don't truly want the thing. To want to become a doctor is to want to maintain a perfect GPA throughout pre-med education, and to spend grueling hours in medical school and residency, and to deal with problems and people far more disgusting than most people have the stomach for, for longer hours than most people have the sanity to endure. You can't truly want the thing without wanting what is necessary to reach it; if you don't want to do what is necessary to reach it, you don't truly want the thing. To want something consequential to happen without consequences, or to want a difficult thing to be attained without difficulty, are not things that can be meaningfully *wanted*, only fantasized about. That being said, there are absolutely meaningful things a person can want in areas such as invention and social justice, whereby things that are unnecessarily difficult now can be made less difficult in the future; even some obstacles which some would call "necessary" might prove to be unnecessary, and be discarded, making things easier for everyone. It is good to want to change things; it is not good to fantasize about things simply being changed for you.

ADMISSION

Even after dispelling the above objections, some readers will find the very concept of acting on "what you want" to be unsavory, out of fear of becoming the selfish person, that prominent villain of popular culture; but one of the most important points of this book is that you should understand and admit your own motivations, and that any conscious decision whatsoever is an assertion of what you want. Once again: one's most noble goals are, at their deepest roots, derived from the most rudimentary, animalistic, stimulus-response motivations – and it is when a large number of these motivations are amalgamated and synthesized that more sophisticated goals emerge. You may be tempted to say to yourself that your highest goals are for the service of some external thing: perhaps in service to civilization, perhaps to contribute to art or science, perhaps in obedience to some god. It certainly sounds attractive to put yourself in service of some immortal, eternal ideal such as this, as if your service to it was something unshakeable, something absolute, a "fixed idea" – but this kind of intellectually-conceived goal is not what lies at the bottom of motivation. Peel away one more layer, and ask yourself the next question: *why* do you want to serve this thing? *Why* do you want to serve this ideal? The service of society, science, or whatever other rationally-conceived concept is not written into your DNA, it is not at the heart of all your decision-making. When you were a child, before you learned to speak, were you in service of this thing? No. You had to *learn* certain things in order to *wish* to serve your ideal – what was it that taught you? What were the rewards and punishments that drove you to your current position? Could it be, perhaps, that doing these things made life *seem* better, or *feel* better for you, and that refraining from them made life *seem* worse, or *feel* worse, in a manner that is perceived by those fundamental parts of your animal being, the ones motivated by pleasure and pain, positive and negative emotion? Once again: could it be that you found yourself unable to sleep, felt a lingering feeling of dread and personal insignificance, or simply seemed to be in a worse place in life when you did not do these great things? And inversely, could it be that you found yourself feeling healthy and satisfied when you actually did do these great things, that you felt that *joie de vivre,* that sensation of being at grace with reality, that sense that you are *doing what you want*, and that *what you want is happening?*

Every motivation has a selfish element, at the bottom of it all. Every decision that you make is made by you; in other words, a decision that you make in the proper sense is one that you judge will be beneficial – that is, beneficial according to *your terms*. It's possible to fail to do this, and to consider yourself hopelessly subjugated by some higher power, either human or superhuman; this is a fast path to both ideological trouble and an unnecessarily negative attitude towards life, an underestimation of your own freedom and a negation of your own identity as a conscious human being.

You should never be afraid to admit to yourself what you want. Now, make sure to think about it carefully, make sure you're not just falling for some kind of rhetoric or sales pitch, and also make sure it's not just some stupid momentary whim – make sure it's realistic and something that would actually make your life, or the life of someone you have an interest in, better in the long term. If it's what you want, it's what you want. Denying the truth about yourself will do nothing but make your life more constrained, and the conditions of life on this planet are already plenty constraining enough. The truth may be the sort of thing that will make others uncomfortable, and it may even make you yourself uncomfortable for a little while, considering what you have "learned" from others – but the truth is the truth, and denying reality will not get you very far in reality. And anyone who would hinder the expression of the truth of what you want to do, who you want to be, is no friend of yours. In spite of how commonplace the theme of "be yourself, it's okay to be different" is in modern media, a great many people are still obsessed with conformity, to the point of forcing certain paths in life onto their children (even if they clearly do not have a positive predisposition towards these paths), or to the point of breaking off a friendship or other relationship unnecessarily (simply because the other person is not enough of a conformist in the field in question). Some people will never be happy unless they create art; should these people be confined to the "normal" life of an accountant or a salesman? A surprising number of people will answer yes; and that includes even some artists who are still living in denial.

Grand designs that stretch beyond the span of one lifetime are no exception to this. If you choose to do something that will affect generations of people in the future, it is still your decision to do this thing. You are still deciding to do it; it is "your interest." Even if you are so non-self-centered that you don't even care about your name being remembered, it is *your activity* which you intend to make real, *your action* which you intend to make, the consequences of which will live on, cascading through time. For that reason, it is still an expression of your life, it is still an exertion of your power, it is still a manifestation of what you want.

On the opposite end, there are small, simple pleasures of the short term which are also a component of what you want. Some people, who have grand designs to change the world, might be tempted by the image of the saint, the ideal of the "pure" person, tempted to adhere strictly to the aesthetic of purity, which is traditionally associated with great figures of the past, of history and mythology. There are more than a few who are unable to imagine that a person can perform great deeds but simultaneously be preoccupied with sexual exploits, or juvenile humor, or other such things which are considered base or vulgar. There was once an incident where Margaret Thatcher was informed, and provided with hard evidence, of Mozart's well-documented penchant for scatological humor; she denied it emphatically, having no interest in any facts which contradicted her idealistic view of the composer. Of those who characterize themselves as holding only the classiest and purest of interests, there are probably a small few who are genuine; but most, being human beings, are probably only self-censoring and self-restricting, denying themselves one or another very classically human kind of pleasure (and many of them proceeding to enjoy it in secret anyway).

MAGNANIMOUS

It may also appear to some readers that the principle of doing what you want conflicts with that moral sensibility which recommends beneficence towards others; but this is not the case. The genuinely magnanimous person does what he wants *par excellence*.

This is easy to prove. Paint in your mind a picture of the genuinely magnanimous person: he works to produce great things, and he gives them generously to others; he forgives offenses against him without resentment; he makes it his goal to, wherever it is feasible, provide something beneficial to those around him who are in need. Now – how does he *feel* about doing all this? Surely, to do these things feels good to him; how could it be otherwise? How else would he be so passionate about his beneficent cause, if it did not stir within him deep feelings of satisfaction and pleasure? If these feelings were not present, the only possible alternative is that he has calculated, on a merely intellectual, non-emotional level, the "correct" ethical behavior, and he performs this behavior rote, *without enjoyment*. But could such a person even be called "genuinely magnanimous"? No, he would be called insincere, a slave to an ideology he does not truly believe in, someone who is only kind and generous begrudgingly, because he feels that he has to behave this way in order to be "correct."

Is it the case, then, that the genuinely magnanimous person is, in the end, motivated only by his pursuit of pleasure? Well, this doesn't sound very magnificent, given the negative connotations that the word "pleasure" sometimes calls to mind. But few people would say that pleasure is bad *per se* – after all, if a person experiences pleasure from being magnanimous, it's reasonable to say that pleasure in this context is not a bad thing, whether you are an egoist or an altruist or anything in between. To feel pleasure from activities which are beneficial to a wide range of human beings, as opposed to your own person exclusively, indicates from the perspective of the altruist that you have a functioning conscience. Meanwhile, to the Nietzschean, to be magnanimous is to be "great-souled" in the literal sense, to overflow with power so prodigiously that utilizing it only for the benefit of a single person, using it for so small and timid a purpose, would be as putting a lamp under a bushel basket – an insult to yourself, even if that single beneficiary is yourself.

In short, there is no inherent contradiction or exclusivity between fulfilling one's own interests and fulfilling the interests of others. Hume writes in his *Enquiry Concerning the Principles of Morals:* "I esteem the man, whose self-love, by whatever means, is so directed as to give him a concern for others, and render him serviceable to society: As I hate or despise him, who has no regard to any thing beyond his own gratifications and enjoyments. In vain would you suggest, that these characters, though seemingly opposite, are, at bottom, the same." If you are a magnanimous person, then to act magnanimously is to do what you want.

SIMPLICITY OF PRINCIPLE

Do what you want. The principle is simple. You can frame it in whatever way is most pleasing to you, whatever way makes the transition between desire and action go the most smoothly. But no matter how you frame the principle, and the acts that proceed from it, always remember what it is at its most fundamental – doing what you want. "I do what I want" – everything else can be derived from that elementary statement. Though the activities required in the execution of what you want might be complex, and though the decisions necessary to determine what you want might be complex, and though formulating a complete expression of what you want might be complex, the principle itself is not complex.

Note the distinction between the simplicity of this principle and the simplicity of an ideology. An ideology is simple in the sense that sets out rules of interpretation concerning the world, and rules of action in the world, which are too limited, too restrictive, and too narrow to account for reality, but which posit themselves as infallible or nigh-infallible nonetheless. The principle is simple in such a way as to be not restrictive, but as broad as you want; and it places the responsibility for interpretation and action solely on you, not on some "authoritative" source of moral judgment to which you "have to" submit. As mentioned, the principle is so broad and so fundamental that it supersedes even the principle of survival – you do not have to survive if you don't want to. And the principle is not a reflection of some person's or organization's preferred rules of behavior, but a primary acknowledgement of one's own existence as a being capable of thought, decision-making, and action; your decisions are your own by definition, and conceptualizing them properly as *your own*, as "what you want," is honesty, accuracy, integrity, and personal identity.

You can dress the simple truth up in whatever frameworks you want. You can express the principle through a thousand different perspectives. You can list a thousand reasons why adhering to the principle is a good idea. You can list a thousand good ideas that are derived from the principle. You can invent as complicated a model as you like to explain the effects of the principle on the world. But don't be confused – the principle is simple.

The next several sections will be "angles" from which the principle of doing what you want could be interpreted. Do not feel obligated to consider any of these "canonical" or "necessary" to working with the principle; the principle stands on its own. If you, reader, find it more useful to view the principle of doing what you want from a different angle than the ones listed below, then by all means, take that angle and make it your own.

REAL SELF

You can think of doing what you want as making your real self real. What is your "real self"? There are two ways of thinking about it.

For those who like thinking in conceptual terms, you can think of your real self as being your ideal self, your self-in-concept. This is your mental image of the "you" who does what you want to do, who has what you want to have, who is what you want to be. This self-in-concept is not a picture of mere fantasy, it is not the imagined outcome of a daydream of winning the lottery or some other such idiocy – it is the image of what you want, not what you merely fantasize about. It is part of the way that you perceive yourself, and it is the way of perceiving yourself that you would like to be true.

When you think judgmentally towards others, when you perceive in yourself a fundamental sort of superiority compared to the flaws of another, it is from the perspective of your imagined ideal self, your self-in-concept, that you do so – even if, in reality, you are as bad as or worse than the person you are judging. And when you think judgmentally towards yourself, reflecting on your own flaws, it is from the perspective of your self-in-concept that you observe these flaws – for what you perceive as flaws are the elements of yourself that are not present in your self-in-concept. When you ask yourself "Why am I doing this? Why do I do this to myself?", you are speaking from the perspective of your self-in-concept, observing your self-in-reality doing something that you don't like.

The way to make your "real self" real in this sense is, of course, to bring this image of yourself into reality, make your self-in-reality line up with your ideal self. This requires a conscious effort, a frequent analysis and critical judgment of your own life, and in particular, an examination of which elements of your ideal self your self-in-reality lacks. Different ways of conceptualizing this will be useful to different people. For some people, it is enough to simply observe these things and say, "these are my flaws," and they will be able to get to work on fixing them. Other people, though, would be tempted by such a phrase into thinking that they have some kind of permanent, unchangeable character flaw; people susceptible to this will benefit better by a more specific formulation, something like "these are the things that, ideally, I wouldn't do." This is a judgment of the situation in your own mind; phrase it in whatever way will most reliably lead you to positive action.

Bear in mind, though: your perception of your self-in-concept at a given moment is not infallible. If you have fallen for an ideology, you will see in place of your self-in-concept the personification of that ideology, the "perfect person" according to some too-simple ideological formula. This character, in lieu of your real ideal self, will be an amalgamation of the orders you have been given by authority figures, presenting you with a distorted picture of what is "absolutely right," rather than a picture of what is right for you. This is one of the reasons why it's essential to learn to avoid the ideological troubles described in Part III – you won't make much progress on your journey if your map is poorly drawn. Refine your self-in-concept by thinking about what you are thinking about; this is a bit complicated, and you will need to get creative in order to frame a process of thinking which also thinks about itself, but anyone can do it. Think of it as a continuation of the methods of learning that you experienced as a child, except now you have enough information to be both the student and the teacher. Once your technique is refined to your satisfaction, and you're confident that you can be a responsible and genuine teacher to yourself, put it into practice; and the outcomes of this practice will help you to refine it even further, and bring an even more refined picture of what you want into reality. The practice of this is essential; fail to practice what you would ideally practice, and you, your "real self," will never become anything more than a thought, a voice in the back of the mind of some jerk – and if that jerk is not doing what you want? Well, too bad, because until and unless you make that change, that jerk will be acting in your stead and reaping what you'll have to sow.

One last thing: don't conceive of your self-in-concept as your "future self" exclusively, i.e., as if it will always be your future self. If you make a habit of imagining to yourself "I'm getting closer, I'm getting there," but you're not actually getting any closer, then your self-conception will either devolve into the realm of fantasy (only fantasizing about the image of your theoretical future self rather than actually intending to make some kind of change) or you will stop trusting your own judgment and come to believe, consciously or subconsciously, that you will never improve.

For those who like thinking in more tangible terms, you could alternately say that your "real self" is your material person. In this sense, your "real self" also isn't real, or at least not very substantial of a character, unless you do what you want. A person who does nothing notable is forgotten by the people of the future. A person who does nothing at all is forgotten by the people of the present. A person who lives a life with absolutely no impact is scarcely different from a person who committed suicide while young, or who was never born. If there is any reality to such a person's existence, what is the evidence of that reality? A headstone, a few records in a database, a few pay stubs and receipts? Hardly worth mentioning. Easily skimmed over by people on their way to do more important things. In the long term, not much of an existence at all. But do not feel that you have to achieve extraordinary feats to avoid this fate: even if what you want to do is not something great or amazing, it is still valuable to do it. Your work will be remembered by those who it helped or inspired, even if it was indirect, even if it was momentary, even if they do not remember your name, or even if they never heard of your name. But to never help anyone, to never create anything, to never do anything to make some small part of the world remotely better? That is a real tragedy and a real failure. That will turn you into the kind of person who would watch *It's a Wonderful Life* and find it to be a cruel, depressing film – how could you think otherwise, if the world without you would be exactly the same as it is now?

These two perspectives, actualization of the ideal self and the pursuit of an existence with more impact in the long term, are entirely compatible. They are two different perspectives through which a person can frame a process of positive transformation, a process of more completely doing what they want.

THE GOLDEN RULE

"Love your neighbor as yourself." An excellent piece of advice, and note the key detail: it is not "above yourself" or "instead of yourself," but "as yourself." There is no loving your neighbor if there is no loving yourself. If you have no love for yourself, then "loving your neighbor as yourself" means having no love for them either. If you have no sense of what would constitute a loving or good action toward yourself, how can you dare to place yourself in another person's shoes, and imagine what is right for them? And in another formulation: "Do unto others as you would have them do unto you." If you have no concept of what would be right to have done unto you, how can you possibly know what is right to do unto others?

Some conscientious people will find it tempting to idealize unselfishness as the highest virtue, but it's entirely possible to have too much of a good thing. Indulging in too much is especially easy if the temptation toward it is increased due to social pressures (to never express your own desire is to never offend anybody) and also if it happens to be the path of least resistance (it takes no effort to develop and act on zero preferences). Thus, people can be tempted toward an excessively selfless identity as either a social posturing technique or out of pure laziness, or both. And what does it look like to be too selfless? Every interest, preference, and desire entails, to some degree, the exclusion or diminishing of the things that they are not. To indicate that something is preferable *to you* is not possible without, in a sense, calling something else inferior. To have the "unselfish" aversion to doing this, to an extreme degree, is to have no interests, preferences, or desires at all; there would be no "you" to speak of, let alone a "you" capable of loving your neighbor, or doing right unto others. In one of her more lucid moments, Rand writes: "To say 'I love you,' one must know first how to say the 'I.'" It is obvious, I hope, that these ideas do not imply that other people should be disregarded wholesale or that altruism is evil; even Stirner writes of his love of every human being: "I love them because love makes *me* happy, I love because love is natural to me, it pleases me." The point is that the golden rule rejects both excessive selfishness *and* excessive selflessness. Treating selflessness as an ideal, rather than one side of an axis that surrounds a happy medium, is saying that the best case would be for there to be no self, no "you," in the first place.

In training for emergency situations, what is the constant theme? In an airplane emergency, put on your own oxygen mask before helping others. In an active shooter situation, if someone refuses to accompany you to the nearest exit, don't waste time trying to convince them, and as you are escaping, don't go out of your way to try to find more people to hypothetically save on the opposite side of the building. If someone is drowning in deep water, and you aren't both a strong swimmer *and* trained for rescue, then you trying to save them will likely result in two people drowning instead of just one. Prioritize saving yourself, and save others only if you can do so without endangering yourself. There are situations where you must refuse to attempt to save someone else, solely for your own sake. This is not heartless. This is not cruel. Self-preservation is fundamental, because if there is no you, there is no good which you can do at all. And in the cases that are not life-or-death, it is even more evident that it is not cruel to have your own identity, to be willing to say "No" to others, to do what you want, even when it contradicts something that somebody else wants, or claims to want.

JUDGMENT

Your judgment should be something that you trust, even when it runs up against the opinions of others. If someone makes a convincing enough argument, your opinion on certain issues may change – this should happen if, and only if, the argument in favor of this new opinion outweighs your attachment to your existing opinion, according to the standards of your judgment. And in the occasional huge mind-blowing revelation, your very methods and principles of judgment might be compelled to change – but only when these changes are necessary according to a yet more fundamental principle of your judgment. You have an ability to think and judge and reason which is, fundamentally, your own. Allowing your own judgment to be dissolved or forgotten, in the name of some so-called virtue, or maintaining some social standing, or simply because you can't be bothered to go to the trouble of dedicating time to critical thought, is the denial of a fundamental part of you, and this will cause you to feel like something is fundamentally wrong or inadequate about you.

In Part III, it was emphasized that you should be willing to admit when you are wrong – you should also be willing to admit when you are right. For starters, you should be willing to admit that you have an actual opinion, yes, even when this opinion entails saying "No" to someone else. To many people this will sound perfectly reasonable, but to some people the thought of instigating any kind of confrontation, even something as small as voicing a difference of opinion, will seem impossible. This might just be due to a person having a nonconfrontational personality, or maybe it's because of a problem with the environment. If you find yourself in a circle of people in whose presence you can't do this, then these people, who would deny you the right to *even have an opinion,* are not your friends, and their approval is not something you have any reason to chase. Reasonable people can have discussions where not everybody agrees on every topic. Reasonable people are able to say "No" to each other, and have conversations that are, in a sense, confrontations, but which are conducted in order to help both parties understand each other's perspective. Reasonable people can have a civil argument, and even if they do not come to a consensus, they can still remain friends afterward. If the people who you talk to are not capable of doing this, you should be aware that *these are not reasonable people.*

Supposing that you do interact with people willing to have a reasonable debate, there is still something of a balancing act. You do not want to constantly automatically minimize your own opinion, and you do not want to constantly automatically minimize the opinions of others; every idea proposed in the course of the argument deserves to be scrutinized with care. It's difficult for people with very different ideas to communicate, but somehow it can be done, and it is done, every day, all the time. Each person, with their own method of thinking, is able to participate in society amidst a huge number of people who think and act very differently than they do, and somehow civilization still functions. It's far from perfect, but still. Doing what you want includes saying what you want; be willing to communicate with other people, and be willing to hear out various opinions, but also, be willing to argue against them – when it's appropriate. If you disagree with a person on a topic, but you know too little about it to defend it without difficulty, it's often better to listen, and gather information for later, rather than starting a confrontation then and there. And above all, be honest. If you do what you want, then you will have the confidence to be honest and open about your opinions, your accounting of events, your tastes, everything.

OVERCOMPLICATION

Beware of conceptualizing simple things in overcomplicated terms. If you don't brush your teeth very often, and you want to start doing it every day, don't think of it as "approaching self-actualization" or "revealing your inmost light" or "taking the next step toward the Übermensch" or "exercising the categorical imperative" or anything involving "enlightenment" or anything complicated like that. Look at what you're actually trying to do here. What you want to do is brush your teeth more often. "Brushing your teeth more often," as part of the broader "doing what you want" – that's it. Simple concepts will suffice.

Don't confuse this recommendation of simple conceptualizations with an ideological stance, by the way. Ideologies attempt to make complex moral issues into simple issues of categorization. Ideology removes nuance. Removing overblown complexity from a description of something like brushing your teeth does not remove any nuance. Saying that you are "manifesting your divine spark" or whatever, in the context of brushing your teeth, is a more complicated sentiment, but it adds no nuance or specificity to the actual thing being described. If you told someone "I'm brushing my teeth more often lately, in order to bring myself closer to the incarnation of the archetypal savior," they would think you're an idiot. Not crazy – just an idiot, someone who fell for some mystical feel-good mumbo jumbo.

TOO OPEN-MINDED

Doing what you want entails removing as many unnecessary "fixed ideas" as possible, in order to open your mind to new possibilities. Is it possible, you may ask, to be too open-minded? Is it possible to see *too many* possibilities for one's direction in life? Yes, there can be too much of a good thing. It's possible to too rapidly discard attachments to ideas, both the bad and the good; and it's possible to too rapidly adopt new attachments to ideas, both the good and the bad. It's possible to navigate life in an unrealistic, unthinking manner and then rationalize it by thinking to oneself something like: "It's a good thing to be open-minded; this is a learning experience." Such a person, however, does not learn in any meaningful sense; they do not intend on becoming more capable of discriminating right from wrong, truth from falsehood, useful from useless. The person goes past what one would call "open-minded," and spirals all the way into becoming mindless.

It's this tactic (or rather, this lack of tactic) of being totally nondiscriminatory concerning information, to basically exhibit no ability to distinguish between true and false, which is the sign that a person is using the ideal of open-mindedness to justify their inadequate attention to the facts of life. In addition to the mentally ill, this can be seen from time to time in people who have an affinity toward "mystical" or "spiritual" thinking, who will agree to almost anything you say that sounds pleasant or positive (possibly due to fear of confrontation), and who are fortunate enough to be in the kind of privileged position where they can disregard a surprisingly large amount of their local reality and not immediately suffer serious consequences. If being open-minded is a willingness to *consider* a wide range of ideas, then this behavior is more like a willingness to *swallow* a wide range of ideas, that is, to agree instantly, without thinking about them. This is naïveté, gullibility, and bizarrely enough, something that can cause a person to become more closed-minded: a willingness to easily accept things could translate into a willingness to easily swallow an ideological stance, in certain cases. Perhaps a person might drift from ideology to ideology on a whim, never actually caring about any one of them very deeply. Or perhaps a person might allow their self-perceived trait of "open-mindedness" to twist into contrarianism, because they say to themselves that they're so open-minded that they're willing to consider the opposite of whatever is currently in fashion; and if "consider" comes to mean "swallow," that could spell a more serious ideological attachment, rationalized to oneself by saying "I'm able to accept it because I'm so open-minded."

It's obvious that a person who attempts to navigate life in this way will have to do a great deal of what you might call doublethink, but the more accurate term is probably "zerothink." It's not so much a deliberate attempt to hold multiple contradictory ideas simultaneously, but rather, a lack of attempting, a naïve desire to simply say yes to everything that sounds nice, to not have to worry about the difficulty of discerning information, which entails saying "No" to people. Holding contradictory opinions is the natural consequence of this, although it's something of an exaggeration to say such a person really "holds" any opinions at all.

DESIRE

"Desire is the root of all evil." The notion that desire should be gotten rid of entirely comes naturally after this maxim, but runs into an immediate problem: the desire to be rid of desire is still a desire. When people cite such maxims as "desire is the root of all evil," they generally mean that it is often a desire of the simplest and easiest type, the most primitive type, which lies at the root of evil. In that case, what is the proper ideal? Not to be free of desire altogether, but to be free of...simple desires? No, that would be ridiculous, since these desires are practical on their own in many circumstances, and they also make up the building blocks of more complex, sophisticated, nuanced desires. Is it to be rid of "bad desires"? No, that's not good enough either, because some desires which we might label as "bad desires" in some circumstances might be acceptable, or even useful, in the right circumstances. The same goes for what we might call "evil desires" – on rare occasion, something that might ordinarily be called evil could be used as a tool for good, such as violence for the sake of self-defense. And it is inadequate for the same reason to seek to have only "good desires," which could in certain circumstances be means or excuses to commit evil. It's obvious that the point is not to try to categorize every conceivable desire into good, bad, or evil, and then refine one's desires accordingly; we do not want to make an indefinitely long, eternally incomplete table of desires, each with an equally long and incomplete series of conditional statements defining their moral status.

It's obvious that the point is to think, to think critically about which desires are worth pursuing at any given time, to not let smaller and more inconsequential desires take priority when there are larger and more consequential desires which should be considered first. When people use "self-centered" as a pejorative, the "self" they are referring to is the set of parts of the self which are insubstantial, short-sighted, too simple – *for long-term plans*. Simple desires have important functions, and there are certainly occasions when one can sit back and act on these desires, when the time is right for leisure – but the time is not always right for leisure. To choose a television show to watch on a whim is likely to end up fine, but to choose a college degree on a whim (or to choose between going to college versus a different life avenue, for that matter) is more dangerous – especially if you insist on clinging unshakably to this whim-generated decision once it's been made. Will your entire lifestyle be determined by something like post-purchase rationalization? To spontaneously insult a person anonymously on the Internet is one thing, but to spontaneously insult a person in real life? The latter could be called "self-centered" in the popular sense of the phrase, because the attitude of giving this insult comes from a "self" (a part of the self, perhaps only a tiny part which only surfaces on rare occasion) which is rude, antisocial, disinterested in beneficial interactions with people; in other words, acting only on dumb instinct, not interested in building long-term bonds, or even being tolerant generally. But this is not the only sense in which a person's actions can be centered on themselves, is it? If a person's desires are good, wouldn't it be good for them to be self-centered? It's peculiar, then, that "self-centered" is used as an insult; maybe those who use it as an insult simply assume that every person's desires are bad or evil by default, and that it's only the need for socialization which spurs people to act good. What a dreary perspective. Of course, it could just be projection.

Do not allow the unimportant to take precedence over the important – the small and superficial can still be a part of you, but only inasmuch as it actually helps you. The root of a great deal of evil does indeed consist of giving too much attention to superficial "self-interests" that aren't actually what you want. It's not that the problem is giving *any* attention, notice; the problem is giving *too much* attention. Acknowledging this is important to admitting the nature and extent of what you want. To try to exist without desire, to be a living thing without interests, is futility, and may lead to strange consequences such as repressed desires leaking out, their existence ignored – what depraved and dangerous results could a person's desire produce if the person refuses to admit, in their conscious moments, that the desire is part of them in the first place? What will they do unconsciously, in a mental state that they refuse to acknowledge afterwards? Nietzsche writes in *Zarathustra*: "Not a few who sought to drive out their devil entered into the swine themselves."

If you say "all who exalt themselves shall be humbled, and all who humble themselves shall be exalted," and you choose to humble yourself – it is because you want to be exalted! This is absolutely elementary, but it's the kind of thing few good Christians would outright admit, as modesty is ever so fashionable. As for those who would admit it, perhaps saying, "I don't want to be exalted in the world of the mundane, but in the kingdom of God" – excellent! An even grander ambition, the desire to be exalted under the strictest criteria and the most consequential setting; one might say, the most *real* setting. I encourage this admission; it is possible that, in the course of time, one's concept of what is real and consequential may change, but the pursuit of *the most real and consequential form of success* is good in principle, at least. This desire is a personal desire, a desire for personal gain; how can there be any denying it? Stirner calls those who deny it "involuntary egoists." If you believe that good deeds are rewarded, and you consequently do good deeds, do you expect anybody to believe that you don't care about the reward at all? When you receive your reward, will you simply cast it aside, as an unimportant nuisance? Of course not! You will reap what you have sown, you will enjoy what you have earned. There are some occasions where being honest is more difficult than being deceitful; but on this occasion, admitting the truth is easier than putting together a convoluted rhetorical contraption to try and paint a portrait of yourself as an impossible creature, a person without desires.

Another unrealistic ideal, often related to the previous one, is the notion of submitting to, or being the instrument of, some kind of supreme, transcendent, universal will, as if such a thing could be known of with certainty. But even given the tenuous assumption that it could be known, to say "I seek not my own will, but the will of the one who sent me" is still to say a contradiction – if it is not your own will to seek this thing, why are you seeking it? You have the option not to; if you don't want to, why go along with it? If someone gave you a task that you found intolerable, that was not aligned with your own will, would you not refuse? Or are you not given the option to refuse, making you a helpless slave to this master? But even a slave retains his individuality, and, being tyrannized with orders that run against his will, would either put up a façade of compliance and wait for a chance to rebel, or, in desperate measures, perform a hunger strike or simply commit suicide. Surely, even if you comply with the will of your master, you must have your own individual will – which may or may not be aligned with his, but is in any case still *your own* will, *your own* desire. For this to not be the case, you would have to be an inanimate object, an instrument in the most literal sense, to be picked up, used, and put down, as a hammer or a saw. In short, the desire to be an instrument to the will of God, or some other "higher power," is still, if you should choose to adopt it, a desire of *your own.*

The concepts of eliminating desire and embracing humility do not point to an ideal worth pursuing to the furthest extremes; only dead matter is devoid of desire. A well-known Buddhist theme occurs here: those who obsessively pursue asceticism are scarcely any different from drunkards and gamblers; they simply dissolve their consciousness (which is the prerequisite for desire) in different ways – both ways being unhelpful. There are some desires that warrant being dissolved and forgotten; others can stay, but should only be catered to occasionally; others should be sought after frequently. Actions made on instinct (whims) are only self-interested according to instinct's tendency to be (what it "thinks" is) self-preserving; actions with real thought behind them can be self-interested in a more nuanced sense, a more sincere manifestation of what you want. The point is to be discerning, to judge between right and wrong without swallowing someone else's rules, even if that "someone else" is a large body of people whose influence makes up a widely-practiced tradition. To obey because of popularity is simply to fall for the bandwagon fallacy.

DEEP THOUGHT

The contemplation of the deepest questions of your existence is a journey that must be undertaken alone. The questions that lie in the deepest depths of your heart cannot be given to you by another person. So, some day or night, you find yourself alone and in peaceful surroundings, a setting conducive to deep thought. What do you do? Concerning this specific exercise, I can recommend general guidelines, but not much more. Too much of it is dependent on the peculiarities of your personal manner of thinking and the details of your situation in life. What I wish to emphasize here is that this is a *solitary* exercise.

The necessity of solitary contemplation comes partially because no one else knows the intricacies of your life (not only your activities, but also your opinions, your likes and dislikes, everything; the deepest and most subtle secrets of your mind) nearly as well as you do – and even if you were to share absolutely everything with some confidante, they still would only be able to understand it as well as you can convey, and only that as well as they can comprehend what you can convey, neither of which will be perfectly well. And it is also partially because these are not the sort of questions about which one *should* receive an answer from someone else, when the intention is to find an answer that you can wholeheartedly rely on – you, a human being, having your innate desire for freedom, for independence, will never be satisfied clinging dependently to someone else's answers to these kinds of questions. There are some circumstances where dependence is acceptable, where being a temporary follower of or worker for someone else is an acceptable cost for a future reward – but this is not one of those circumstances. This is your very soul looking into itself, making the fundamental judgments of good, bad, and evil, and venturing into unexplored realms of thought in order to answer those frightening questions of life and death; the development of *you* at the most fundamental level is not the occasion to defer to someone else's ideas, and certainly not to cling to them. Even in this book, the best I can convey to you are these basic principles which will make the self-evaluation process go more smoothly, elucidate the elements of the exercise, and broadly inform the method. I cannot pretend to give a more specific prescription.

The types of questions to ask yourself in these moments of serious introspection concern the topics that have already been explained in this book, encompassing suicide, what you want, who you are, and the rest, all being tightly interlinked with each other. Progressing towards an answer to one question of this depth will inform all related questions. And of course, you should also ask questions pertinent to your own specific concerns. What has your life consisted of so far? Where are you now? What do you want? How will you get it? And so on. To answer these questions properly, especially to the person who has not really considered such things before, will require a willingness to *explicitly admit the truth,* to be honest with yourself in a way that perhaps one has never been before. How easy it is to lie, and to lie by omission by deferring these questions, by kicking them out of your head before they are even fully articulated! There are so many anxieties and difficult questions which are so easy to brush off, even in moments of deep thought, as being "too difficult for now," as something "for another time." But postponing them for another time will do nothing but perpetuate the present, it will only keep you the same distance from what you want; and invariably, progressing towards what you want will become more difficult as aging takes its toll. The kinds of questions that actually can be postponed, e.g., difficult political or social questions that you might feel the need to have an opinion on, can wait (for those who are still in the formative stages of determining what they want, at least). Establishing an identity should come first; to say that "you" have an opinion before you know who "you" are is putting the cart before the horse.

And one more thing: to confirm that the deep questions that you ask yourself are decisively answered, it's best to articulate the conclusions you reach by writing them down somewhere. It's surprisingly easy to think to yourself that you have a solid, concrete idea, only to try to write it down and realize that it's more of a vague, uncertain feeling. To formulate your ideas in actual words is essential to understanding their real extent, consistency, and comprehensibility.

POSSIBLE ANSWERS

The fact of mortality is every human being's fundamental limitation, and the most effective Answers are those that overcome this limitation. If a human being does nothing for the rest of their life, committing suicide earlier produces the same long-term outcome from the individual perspective as dying of old age later – how to insure against this? By contributing to the future, of course. To contribute to the future of the human race, and life in general, is the kind of goal which allows something of a person's existence to persist for longer than their life; it makes a person's existence into something more permanent than that of the person who is merely a passenger in life, merely along for the ride. Earlier, it was said that an Answer is the discovery of that which is so important that suicide can be forgotten, or at least postponed, until it is achieved; since death will be the outcome for the individual in any case, simply *having* something which can be considered a priority in the long run entails thinking about the external world, about other people and about the future, about that which will exist after one's own death.

The most obvious way to contribute to the future is parenthood. This is what you might call the "default" Answer to the Question, reproduction being a fundamental characteristic of life. The nature of the contribution to the future is obvious; the person who procreates ensures the very existence of the next generation, the contribution of their individual genes to the next generation, and typically, the conveyance of one's knowledge and wisdom via child-rearing to the next generation. One's descendants are the products of one's own life in the most literal sense, proof of one's existence which lasts as long as one's descendants are willing to keep at it.

Just because it is the simplest or most obvious Answer, however, does not mean that it is the best for everyone. Some people are well-disposed toward parenthood; others are very badly-disposed toward it. Some people's personalities lend themselves very poorly toward close interpersonal relationships, and some such person who becomes a parent because they think they "have to" may end up seeing their spouse and children with total indifference, or even revulsion. Some people will feel very constrained in such a close relationship as that of a nuclear family, too constrained, so constrained that they would go to considerable lengths to escape this position of being stuck with a bunch of people that they don't care about. Such people are not inherently "worse people" on account of their personalities, but they are very likely to be worse parents. Some people simply do not want to become parents, even if other people or the media fool them into thinking they do. Luckily, thanks to technological advances, sperm and egg donation now exist as options, allowing those who want to contribute their genes to the future to do so without the difficulty of parenting – if, of course, their genetic qualities are in demand.

Aside from parenthood, there are many ways to contribute to the future of the species. The most self-evident examples are the extraordinary ones: the great artists, leaders, inventors, scientists, and so on, the ones whose names are written in the history books. The artist contributes to the future by expressing that which has never been expressed before, expanding the realm of the human experience. The artist looks just under the surface of public consciousness, sees that which is just below the surface, that which is vaguely known but not properly acknowledged – and pulls it out, and shows it to the people: "Here it is! Look at it!" The artist presents images of the world to the people, images of the beautiful, the ugly, the remarkable, the mundane, the concrete, the abstract, anything which stirs minds and hearts, but especially the *new*. All of this can be achieved through a huge number of different artistic media, and an infinite number of concepts – a field of work all the time expanding, making the human experience broader, richer, fuller. The leader contributes to the future by bringing up something like an organization or civilization, large or small, and ensuring that its functions run smoothly and that the people who populate it will prosper. The inventor contributes to the future by creating new technologies or methods, which make life easier or more enjoyable for the people, one way or another. The scientist contributes to the future by extending the field of human knowledge, informing every profession which has use for it: inventors and doctors, obviously, but also engineers, technicians, and many other workers.

Though not as glamorous as the great artists or inventors, workers should certainly not be forgotten as contributors to the future, for they contribute to the *immediate* future, and often the longer term as well. A well-built piece of architecture will stand for centuries, even millennia, and it is not only the architect and commissioner who create such a thing, but every construction worker laying bricks, pouring concrete, arranging the plumbing and HVAC and electrical system, etc. The honest, efficient, no-nonsense worker deserves respect, as an indispensable part of the community. Where workers like this are hard to come by, people suffer. There are also the white-collar workers, occupying offices across the world, who also contribute to the future. The effective use of sophisticated technology often requires a lot of support on many levels, and someone must keep the electronic wheels turning in order to keep the large systems we take for granted from grinding to a halt. There are many kinds of information that everyone wants but few people know how to get; using technical expertise to acquire and convey this information is another way of contributing – especially when the results are shared with the public, and the body of public knowledge increases as a result.

Humble forms of work are also very important, but, of course, not everyone is suited for a humble job. Some people will be unsatisfied by a humble line of work, requiring something different, perhaps something more advanced; others will not be satisfied as workers at all, and will only find happiness as an artist, a leader, or some other type of prominent or special character. Modesty is reasonable and fashionable, but false modesty is a patronizing lie to others, and a restriction on oneself.

Being bold is often better: if not in day-to-day conversation, then in one's actions, one's creations, one's activities toward the positive changing of the world. Artists and thinkers can be obscure but still great; sometimes history will vindicate them, elevating them from obscure to known, or at least to less-obscure; but none of these are the careful ones, the ones playing it safe, the ones doing everything according to that which people will already accept, the ones sticking to the status quo. Fortune favors the bold. If you trust your convictions, if you trust your own judgments regarding what is best for you in life, be bold with them, decisive, active. Be what the passive and ineffectual would call reckless, do what they would be afraid to do – not actual recklessness, but movement, activity, vivacity. In fact, it's best to be bold in the pursuit of what you want even given the possibility of your convictions and your ideas about what you want being *wrong* – as long as you're using your brain and not merely jumping haphazardly into great risk, odds are good that even if things turn out for the worse, you will be able to recognize your mistakes and correct them without suffering serious consequences, all the while improving your understanding of the world and gaining a more accurate bearing toward what you want. Even in the unlikely case that something truly catastrophic happens in the course of your pursuit, and you find yourself severely hindered in your ability to pursue what you want, others will have the ability to learn from your mistake and not make it themselves. Once again, this is not to advocate real recklessness and wanton destruction; rushing into such things on the grounds that "even if I'm in the wrong, it will be good because other people will learn from it" is just the broken-window fallacy. What this really applies to is the kind of path in life that a large number of people would like to aspire towards, but which hasn't been tried a certain way yet; if pursuing it decisively and intelligently still ends in catastrophe, that's an educational experience for the world to write down in the history books, and the people of the future will be all the wiser in avoiding it. After all, if you aren't the first to try it, someone else will be – and do you trust that other person to not foul it up even worse?

JOB

If you were not born very rich, odds are very high that you will want to have a job of some sort; that is, that your overall plan for what you want will include you working for a living. If this is the case, then as for the relationship between your job and what exactly you want, there are three options. First, have a job in which you do what you want. Second, have a job that pays, and use the money to finance what you want. Third, suffer.

The first option is the best, if you can manage it; but it's difficult and risky. This is the option which can lead people to live extraordinary lives, contributing with great passion to a cause that they care about, and getting paid for it as a bonus. It's people like this who can appreciate the phrase "If you do what you love, you'll never work a day in your life." Working full-time on what you want will lead to great achievements that you won't be able to reach otherwise. But there are difficulties and risks, some of which may actually render this path impracticable in certain cases. Maybe what you want isn't something that you can get paid for in the first place. Maybe getting paid for what you want is only possible under some extremely variable condition, like fame. Maybe you would need to start a business from the ground up in order to have what you want be your job, and you would need startup capital that you don't have. Are the risks worth it? Are you up to the challenge? This is what you will need to decide. Higher risk, higher reward.

The second option is also good, though not as impressive as the first. It's the relatively safe option, the option that is very likely to be sustainable long-term, but which has certain drawbacks. If your work isn't what you want in and of itself, it had better at least be something you're comfortable doing a lot of, most days of your life, for a long time. Don't despair at this concept; our hunter-gatherer ancestors had to hunt and gather a lot, most days of their life, for a long time. Just recognize what you're getting into. And try different things; if you work for a large organization, you might have the opportunity to rotate to different branches, doing different kinds of work, without the risk and annoyance of applying to new job after new job. Employers have realized that employees who hate their jobs tend to do them badly; they won't begrudge you for moving around a little before you find the kind of job you're comfortable sticking with long-term.

The third option is the worst, obviously. If you have a job and it's not getting you any closer to what you want, then what's the point? Survival? If your job pays so little and/or is so mentally taxing that survival with it is no better than survival without it, something's gone very wrong, and it's time to find another job, or move to a different city, or something. Maybe even look into alternate ways of getting income, without having a regular job.

One way of reaching the third option is finding yourself in a job that you dislike, where you feel that you're hopelessly stuck, and trying to make yourself love it. This is a very effective way to suffer immensely. Putting yourself in a position where you think you "have to" be, and then telling yourself it's what you wanted all along? It's putting a square peg into a round hole. It doesn't work. Try to hammer it in, and something's going to break. To avoid this, first of all, understand your situation. Some people might think their job "has to" be their passion, and if it isn't, their job is unacceptable and they should hate it – but this isn't the case. You can have a job that's just a source of income. You do work, you get paid, and you use that money to acquire what you want. That's the second option, which is fine. Then again, there are some people out there who can't tolerate that, who really do *need* their job to be their passion – these people have more incentive to take the risk of the first option, and aspire to a full-time project which will satisfy them.

Similarly, make sure that you're not thinking one-dimensionally about your career prospects. If you go for the second option, and you have the idea of "I'm here to make money" stuck in your head, you might end up going too far, pursuing money for its own sake and forgetting about what you want. For a 20% increase in salary, would you submit to a job that's twice as difficult? Is the extra mental stress something you're willing to take on as a part of your plan for what you want? Does that extra bit of money actually make that alteration to your life worthwhile? The same goes for those who would go after "career advancement" and "prestige." There are lots of targets in life that you can chase after that sound very nice, titles and offices and contacts and big names that seem very impressive – but if they're not what you want, don't feel obligated to chase after them.

INACTION AND FANTASIZING

Concerning both the execution of what you want and the experimentation necessary to determine what you want in the first place, it's important to be decisive so that you will reach your goals sooner rather than later.

There are many people who have in their mind a fantasy about what they want, and who love to occupy their minds by contemplating what it would be like to achieve what they want – but who have no intention of actually achieving it. This is a troublesome form of laziness that disguises itself by pretending to be on the brink of some grand achievement. Using this method, a person might try to fool themselves into thinking that they have utility, that they have integrity as a person with goals, that their life has a purpose, and that they're "finally" about to begin the execution of their plan. But they have no real intention of beginning any such thing. Their only wish is to continue fantasizing, to continue letting their imaginations run wild, to remain indefinitely at the point of "just about to begin" and to go no further. What they desire is not the actual achievement of anything, but the *image* of themselves achieving something, even if that image only appears in a daydream. It is very possible to say "I will do it tomorrow" every single day for years and years, without moving an inch closer to doing such-and-such thing, without even intending to do it tomorrow or any other day, only savoring the sensation of saying "I will do it tomorrow" again and again.

The above habit, the habit of fake planning and fake fantasizing (fantasizing about things that will never become reality) is a path to an incredibly boring life. Whenever a person is shaken out of their daydreaming, they will observe just how little progress they have made, just how uninteresting their life actually is outside of their daydreams. But it is possible to transmute this type of desire from a fake into the real thing. To fantasize about achieving something and then to actually achieve it – that is the transformation of a dream into reality. Is there any greater satisfaction? For those who fantasize about that which is actually achievable (that is, those who have relatively healthy habits of fantasizing), decisive action is often the only missing ingredient. But it is the deal-breaker; it is the most critical ingredient.

Recall the behavior, described in Part II, of people who would wait "until the mood strikes them" or "until they feel like it" before doing the things that they want. This is an obvious and unnecessary obstacle, another excuse for inaction, but it's also an implicit clinging to a "you have to." What the chronic procrastinator is waiting for is for something outside their control, either their own emotions or some external party, to force them into action. Imagine that! Imagine having something that you desperately want to do, and then spiting yourself by refusing to do it until something commands you, until something demands: "You have to!" This is another manifestation of the phenomenon mentioned in Part III, of people who want to be enslaved, who want to be ordered around, who want their decisions to be made for them, who want to have a singular and simple path forward, devoid of the necessity for conscious choice. How does it happen that a person develops a mindset like this? Perhaps they weren't raised quite right, and only ever did actually productive things when they were ordered to by their parents or teachers under threat of punishment, never being shown or taught that these things have actual benefit, never conceiving of them as things worth doing voluntarily. If that happens to be the case for you, though, don't be too quick to use it as an excuse – self-psychoanalysis isn't a useful tool if you only use it to excuse inaction. The past can't be changed, but there is more to you than your past.

REWARD

Looking at the big picture, what you want will likely entail not just a single goal, but a whole lifestyle; you may find the perfect job or task or role, but what will you do when you are finished for the day? Will you immediately go to sleep, and get to work immediately upon waking up, spending your entire consciousness on this one thing? A tiny number of people might be able to tolerate this; for the rest, for those who intend to do more than one thing with their time, doing what you want entails both work and rest. Some people might cringe at the thought of performing great and important work, then returning home and watching some juvenile TV program or some other simple indulgence. It might seem inconsistent, but in the end, does it actually matter? "A foolish consistency is the hobgoblin of little minds," writes Emerson; and the present subject is only aesthetic inconsistency, the most inconsequential kind of inconsistency. Stephen Hawking was a fan of Jim Carrey and Larry the Cable Guy; not to mention his many TV cameos on sitcoms and such. Mozart was mentioned in an earlier section; Frank Zappa is yet another well-known example. It is not at all difficult to find eccentrics among extraordinary people. And if they can be eccentric, the less extraordinary can be as well. Why not?

Following this, and recalling the fact that to want something is to want everything that it entails, it's important to have a plan in mind for rest and relaxation, the short-term "rewards" that serve as contrast to the more important "work." The brain's perception of reward occurs in a relative way, as anyone who has taken even a cursory glance at the psychology of addiction is aware. A constant exposure to some kind of stimulus, which might otherwise be a "reward" stimulus, causes it to cease to feel rewarding. There is no pleasure in a "reward" activity unless it is preceded by some kind of "non-reward" from which it can be differentiated. If what you want involves receiving pleasure from a reward, then part of what you want entails doing things other than constantly indulging in "reward" behavior. Even if, by whatever means, you are able to get by without a job, you will not be able to make yourself happy simply by bombarding yourself with food and entertainment. The reason is obvious: "reward" activity of this kind has rapidly diminishing returns.

This is not to say that the "non-reward" activity can't or shouldn't be "rewarding" in a certain sense – being "rewarding" is different from being a "reward." Cooking a delicious meal is a rewarding task; eating a delicious meal is a reward. If you are not hungry, even your favorite foods will have no flavor. If you have found a food that you especially like, do you stuff yourself with it every hour of every day? Of course not; you would get fat, or make yourself sick, or lose your enjoyment for it, or all three.

Imagine a person who is working a tedious and difficult job that they hate, working long hours and only having a little bit of time to rest at home. They spend this time watching TV, relaxing their mind as much as possible during those precious moments when a supervisor is not breathing down their neck. This person is able to perceive these moments of relaxation as a "reward." On Saturday, this person still craves the ability to watch TV during every available hour – so they do. But after a couple of hours, it's not so much fun anymore; they continue doing it nonetheless, perhaps hoping that it will become fun again. When 10:00 PM comes around, the person wakes up from their stupor, realizing, not happily, that they just did nothing for an entire day. Their "relaxing," their "reward," wasn't actually very relaxing or enjoyable. On Sunday, this person does all of the chores and errands they had meant to do on Saturday, occupying several hours of their day in doing so, and eventually settles down into watching TV that evening – and all of a sudden, it's a lot more enjoyable. The physical and mental effort of these errands were not particularly high, but they were something. Having the brain and the body do *something* is infinitely better than having them do *nothing*, not only for practical reasons (e.g., the utility of taking care of the errands in question) but for even more rudimentary self-serving reasons, for ensuring that one's pleasures are actually pleasurable. Now, while our hero can find the means to enjoy their reward, their job is nonetheless tedious and oppressive. Suppose they find another job, a better job, tasked with a different sort of work and being managed differently, for the better. The situation changes such that the employee is not just using their attention to perform repetitive, menial tasks, but properly using their brain to solve problems, and they are also not being micromanaged or otherwise troubled with a needlessly difficult work environment. Now this worker can return home not exhausted, but satisfied, proud of their work in some way; their work may not truly be their "passion," it may not be in itself what they want, but that's not an issue. With less exhaustion and more mental clarity, this person will not only be able to continue enjoying their favorite pleasures (and with a happier conscience, at that), but will also find more time and better ability to use the funds from this job to do what they want.

PREREQUISITES

There is no need to "force yourself" or "prime yourself" or "mentally prepare yourself" to do such-and-such thing. Just do what you want.

There is no need to imagine that you need some kind of ethereal substance, such as "discipline," "motivation," or "determination," which you must have in sufficient quantities to do what you want. These words do not indicate prerequisites, things needed *before* a certain action; these are words used to describe a person's actions *after* the action has been performed. A person who works tirelessly toward a goal is said to be determined, to "have determination," to "have motivation," and this is said only *after* they have achieved the goal. If you want these terms to describe you, then just do what you want.

Due to the English structure of phrases like "this person had to have a lot of discipline to do that," a literal interpretation can give the false impression that a person needs to be in a particular mental state in order to do certain things. Some people, getting this idea stuck in their minds, could, in almost any circumstance, refuse to do what they want on the grounds that they are "not in the mood to do it" or some such nonsense, and they will intend to wait until they are "in the mood." They will wait and wait, but the "mood," or the "motivation," or whatever they tell themselves they are missing, will never arrive. What exactly is this person waiting for? If a person begins waiting in this sense, procrastinating on goals that they set themselves, there will be no instigator to action, no sudden moment of inspiration, no positive and energetic sensation which waiting will eventually produce in their mind. Waiting in this sense will produce nothing except guilt, negative emotion. Granted, negative emotion such as guilt and self-loathing *can* spur a person into action. But is this the pattern by which you wish to live your life? Will you never perform any action until your shame concerning your inaction has grown so great that you can no longer bear it? Will you then, once you have succeeded in achieving something at the spur of your self-hatred, proceed to start waiting once again, doing absolutely nothing once again, until the sense of guilt once again becomes overwhelming? Is this cycle an attractive way of life? No. If you find yourself in this kind of cycle, waiting for yourself to feel guilty enough to act, here's a tip: you will find that doing things *before* you feel weary of waiting for yourself to do them feels good, and the opposite feels bad. Even if only for the sake of pure pleasure, *do what you want,* early and often.

Similarly, don't be too keen to put off actions because you think you have not "trained yourself" sufficiently to do them. There are some things that you do need to train yourself to do – but some things you already know you are able to do. The same for "preparing yourself." There are some things you do need to prepare yourself for – but there are some things you know you are able to do right now. "Training" and "preparing" are words with a positive, healthy, prudent sound; a person can be tempted to put off what they want in favor of smaller "training" or "preparing" activities, but this is just laziness in disguise. You should not need to give yourself a motivational speech in the mirror to prepare to unload the dishwasher. You should not need to brush your teeth one tooth at a time, with a 5-minute break between each, to train for the day in the future when you will brush your teeth all in one sitting. Do not set up unnecessary obstacles for yourself in this way. Make the transition between noticing that you want to do something and doing it to be as seamless, smooth, and fast as possible. Avoid the additional mental overhead of second-guessing yourself; if you already know how to do something, if you know you are able to do it, and especially if *you've done it before*, then just do it.

Concerning those things that actually do require some sort of training, be careful how you conceptualize the act. Don't think of "training yourself" or "convincing yourself" as you think of a master training a pet, or a teacher convincing an unwilling student. Good habits are formed by doing things repeatedly, and skills are gained with practice. Things done repeatedly in order to reach a goal or change the state of your life can be, and often are, within the scope of what you want; not every change is a coercion, not every change is something forced upon you. If a person happens to go through their entire youth without voluntarily training themselves in any skill or good habit, if their entire life has been guided by adults giving them routines to practice and forcing them into performing work over and over again, they may despise repetitive action categorically, and may think of any attempt at "training themselves" as self-tyranny and unnecessary restriction. If this is your situation, know that practice is necessary to become good at anything, and that if being good at something is part of what you want, practice is part of what you want; and unlike practicing what you do not want under someone else's orders, practicing what you want for your own sake feels good.

INSTRUCTION

There are many arts which, like cooking, are taught by instruction; but the instruction is not the art. If you are following a recipe, and manage to do so very precisely, but the food turns out burnt on the outside and raw on the inside, it doesn't matter how precisely you were following the recipe; the heat must have been too high. The fact that you cooked it at the exact heat and for the exact amount of time specified by the recipe, and the fact that you used the exact ingredients and proportions specified in the recipe, and the fact that you are using the same equipment as the instructor, down to the same pan and food thermometer, do not matter. If it turned out badly, it turned out badly. If the end result is not what you want, something must change. Whether this recipe was provided to you by a world-famous chef or by your own grandmother, the fact remains that you must change something in order to get what you want. Sanctifying the recipe, exactly as it is, will only give you the same unsatisfactory result every time. That is not to say the recipe is useless, of course; it exists to provide you with useful information, a general or introductory description of how the thing is done, or perhaps of how it *was* done by someone at some point in the past – but if the end result is not what you want, it doesn't matter how closely you've followed the recipe. Something will have to change, and you will have to use your brain, use some trial and error, and figure out for yourself exactly what to keep, what to add, and what to remove.

So it goes with all kinds of other arts: painting, woodworking, playing music, bodybuilding, wrestling, motorcycle maintenance, and so on, even beyond the material arts and into the concept of instruction in general. Exceptions to this are very few (namely, where the outcome desired is something very specific that follows immediately and tangibly from carrying out very particular instructions, such as doing your taxes). If you have a set of instructions before you, either invented by yourself or received from someone else, and following them brings you neither knowledge nor pleasure nor productivity, are they worth following? It could be that following them precisely is clearly not worth it – but perhaps some modifications can be made to these instructions to suit your situation. Some items might be discarded, others might be added, others reinterpreted and followed in a different sense; perhaps the entire set of instructions is only worth throwing away, if it turns out that there is truly not an ounce of benefit to be found in following them. If you intend to follow something, follow whatever works, whatever gets the job done, whatever brings the result that you want.

Applying this critical attention is easy for instructions that you do not feel personally attached to, but those that you *are* attached to should not be exempt from critical thought – in fact, to cure yourself of your biases, the ones you are the most attached to should be the *most* thoroughly scrutinized. Some readers may be thinking to themselves, "Aha, well, it's a good thing I've already discovered the path to achieving what I want! All I need to do is this and that..." But this too could be wrong. It is possible to deceive yourself by speaking and thinking of grand concepts, using the most elegant words – and simply inserting, as the key to achieving everything, whatever seems most attractive to you in-the-moment. Perhaps this thing is the status quo, or perhaps a pretty new thing you have just come across, or perhaps an *ugly* new thing, something that someone might call "the cruel truth about this world." The crux of this deception is this clinging, this fixing of an idea, this fast-setting adhesion to an idea, this *de facto* assumption of an idea as being the ultimate truth, the last key to victory, the infallible path to perfection. Anything can be described in magnificent terms. You can set up a grand ideological arrangement for anything; if you are a religious person, you are likely of the opinion that most religions other than yours do this very thing. Everything in this world is finite and imperfect; treat nothing as if it were perfect, and be especially careful not to *dodge your own thought process* by treating something in practice as if it were perfect while simply not thinking about whether it actually is. Never bury yourself in something just because it appears good, even when it is your own creation. Keep a critical eye on everything, and especially on your own experiments and endeavors – because merely saying to yourself that something is "your own," that something is "what you want," might tempt you to believe that it is unquestionably perfect for you.

LITERARY EXAMPLES

Many examples of not doing what you want have been given in Parts I-III of this book; let us add a few well-known examples from literature. Kafka's masterwork, *The Trial,* is a portrait of a man who does not do what he wants. In this dark comedy, the protagonist sabotages himself at every turn, while also being thrown about by person after person, each new character claiming to have the perfect solution by which he should confront his trial. Josef K. attempts to solve the insoluble problem of his trial, in a direct allegory for a person attempting to solve the equally insoluble problem of his own mortality.

As an example of K.'s foolishness, he wields great power, even over the incomprehensible and remote Court, but refuses to use it. Simply by speaking a few words of fact in front of certain members of the Court, two of his previous tormentors are severely disciplined – flogged, in fact. If he can exert this much influence accidentally, imagine what he could have been capable of had he used his power deliberately. But K. does not wish to use his power deliberately; he cringes at the thought of becoming an inconvenience to others, even to those who have invaded his home, stolen his food, and refused to show any proof of legitimacy of their operation. Earlier in the story, when K. is first accosted in his home, he wishes to contact the local public prosecutor, to which the supervising inspector nonchalantly approves – but once granted this permission, K. abruptly refuses to do the very thing he wanted to do! And for what reason? Some nonsensical, contrarian form of spite, a childish instinctual reaction to refuse anything proposed by this adversarial unknown person.

Ironically, K.'s preoccupation with his trial only seems to make his situation worse, probably because the trial really doesn't have much impact on his life (in the mortality interpretation, K.'s response is much like a person constantly obsessing over the thought of death rather than maintaining a healthy general awareness of it). He is told as much after his initial "arrest," and again after the episode with the magistrate (during which K. also remained in a state of more or less complete freedom). The only apparent effects of the trial are the effects of other people talking *about* the trial – nothing official comes from the Court itself. He has absolutely no way of measuring his success or failure in terms of improving the circumstances of his trial, but nonetheless, he spends a great deal of mental energy poring over it.

Even when K.'s situation is very explicitly revealed to him by the priest, he still takes no action. In the allegorical story-within-the-story, the protagonist neither fights his way past the gatekeeper nor leaves the area to do something else with his life, but sits and waits and exchanges useless information. K. learns nothing from this. When the executioners come for K., he goes with them complicitly. But it is not complicity in death that is K.'s central flaw; death is unavoidable, one has no choice but to be complicit in it. His flaw is his complicity in his lack of life. The fact that he was executed on his 31st birthday, one year after his initial arrest, is totally arbitrary. The outcome would have been equivalent if he had remained as he was, doing nothing for, instead of one year, 20, 40, or 60 years instead.

Another excellent illustration of someone who refuses to do what he wants is Dostoyevsky's *Notes from Underground.* The Underground Man is much more self-aware than K., explicitly spelling out his character flaws in his masochistic, misanthropic diatribes. He despises his own consciousness for giving him the ability to reject "the sublime and beautiful," and treats the fact of his squalid, meager existence as a consequence of the fact that he is given the mere *option* to exist in such a way. He is highly intelligent, but he primarily uses his ability to concoct elaborate arguments in his own head, to the ends of denouncing himself, humanity, fate, or some such; he only puts his intelligence to what you might call "productive" use on the occasions when a sadistic whim strikes him. He is the type of person to spend months and years seething about tiny perceived slights, and to fantasize obsessively about what else might have happened and how he could, in his imagination at least, revenge himself. He is "underground," disconnected from other people, alternating between feeling envious of them and feeling superior to them.

The Underground Man was not downtrodden from the start; he had not just his high intelligence on his side, but was also given several chances, several advantages, all of which he refused. His arguments alternate between self-righteously justifying his hopeless position and self-loathingly explaining the exact reasons why his choices led to his detriment. It's not that he's in denial the facts of his situation, and it's not even that he doesn't care (in fact, he seems to care extremely intensely) – it's just that he's not doing anything about it. He consistently lets any whim of his take complete control once it has struck him; and once it has, he sticks to it, he follows it unfailingly, even if it should cause him nothing but misery afterwards, and even if he knows this in advance. He offers no explanation as to why he refused the high-status job that he had lined up for him after he made his way to the top of his class (and this he only did to spite the other students), nor as to why he chose to emotionally abuse his only friend, nor as to why he made several other egregiously self-defeating decisions. Even throughout the short time covered by the book's second part, he is given multiple chances to redeem himself – he spits on each opportunity and only uses the occasions for petty cruelty. No reason is given; his effective position is that whenever a whim strikes him, he must obey, even when he is in a conscientious mood and knows what he wants, and knows that this whim is not what he wants – he insists on obeying.

Another variation appears in Gogol's short story *The Overcoat*. The protagonist, one way or another, has completely institutionalized himself, dedicating his entire consciousness to his civil service job as a copyist. He displays absolutely no interests beyond copying documents, and the prospect of the slightest novelty or variation anywhere in his life horrifies him. Beneath his apparent complacency with monotony is an actual personality, complete with genuine emotions and desires - it is heavily repressed, but revealed at a few key points throughout the story, most dramatically during the last days of his fever. Intriguingly, once he is forced into a situation where his survival necessitates doing something different with his life, how much more vivaciousness does he suddenly display! Having no option but to actually do something, how pleasant he finds it is to change things, to act with thought and intention, to break the monotony! This is not an uncommon phenomenon. A person who isn't doing much with their life could easily find themselves downright *excited* if they suddenly feel that they are forced to do something, that they have to make things better for once (e.g., if they have an unexpected visitor and suddenly have to clean their filthy home). The fact that pleasure that can come from unexpected change, even *unwanted* change, shows that hope still exists for even those who seem to have reduced themselves entirely to a tedious, useless life. But in this particular story, a life that had been for so long utterly devoid of activity, a personality so infrequently manifested over so many years, has resulted in serious damage; his brief period of improvement was not enough to rid him of his deep-seated insecurity and vulnerability, and two bad days in a row are enough to finish him off. It was perpetually failing to do what he wanted which made him weak; his development of a false personality, the lie that he actually *did* like his monotonous and empty life, signed his death warrant.

RECOGNITION

Hopefully, the preceding sections and their various angles have helped the reader to understand what I mean when I say "do what you want." The final sections of this book contain some ideas that are not so easily palatable if the principle is not clear to the reader, and especially if the benefits of doing what you want have not been understood through immediate, direct experience. To help with this most important aspect, here are some indicators of success, some signs that you are, in fact, doing what you want – to most readers, these signs will be obvious indicators of success, but there may be some readers who have simply never thought critically about such things before, or never really tried to consciously analyze their life experiences according to these criteria. But even to those who read these things as obvious, a reminder may still be in order – it's very possible to understand a thing and consider it obvious when it is laid out on paper, but to forget entirely about these things in practice, acting identically to a person who doesn't know the difference between a good outcome and a bad one.

The most important indicator of doing what you want is a sense of balance: Balance between the hardy pleasure of working and the comfortable pleasure of relaxation, balance between familiarity and novelty, balance between thinking and acting. When a day consists of a wide variety of physical and mental experiences, the body gets exercise and so does the brain. Conspicuously absent are significantly unbalanced sensations: the muted sensation of doing absolutely nothing for a long period, the dull ache of occupying your entire day doing the same exact thing over and over again, the neurotic frenzy of trying to defeat your boredom with distraction after distraction, the fury of submerging your consciousness in a juicy and violent news story, the disproportionate anger at a minor inconvenience (which seems major when you are trying not to think at all), the self-loathing, self-sustaining, almost *self-indulgent* guilt and shame of failing to do something you genuinely wanted to do, etc.

There is something of a "natural" sensation that comes with doing what you want, as if doing all these things is as natural for you as building a dam is for a beaver, or chasing a rabbit is for a fox, as if you had the potential within you all along to do what is "destined" for you; as if you had been before merely sleeping, merely distracted by things that really aren't very attractive in the first place, now that you think about it. There is a sensation that everything is in order, that everything that is occurring is simply the natural consequence of how things are, that all is well – relatively, at least.

If you are the sort of person who wastes a lot of time while accumulating a large number of unfinished tasks, and you clear your backlog after deciding one day to start doing what you want, you will notice that you suddenly have a surprisingly large quantity of free time – time that was not free previously, time that you previously completely filled up by distracting yourself from the things you actually wanted to do. If you pay attention, if you intend to use each hour for a productive purpose, it might even seem like you have *too much time* available, so much time that it's difficult to fill it all with activity. This is a very good problem to have! There is tremendous, rapid progress you can make towards every goal or interest of yours, by fully capitalizing on your free time – and, by doing so, making it truly your *free time* rather than *time to kill*. Inversely, if you wake up in the morning and promptly distract yourself for 16 hours before deciding to act like a conscious person, you'll find that your free time is exhausted before you've even started using it, and that it's practically time for bed already.

Well, all this is obvious enough. Depending on your personality type, there may be troublesome sensations and situations of other sorts that you will find to be conspicuously absent when doing what you want, and life will feel conspicuously good in other ways. In fact, once you start paying attention, the perceptions of "reward" and "punishment" associated with doing what you want and not doing what you want can sometimes even seem disproportionate to the situation – when you do what you want, it may seem as if good things are happening to you in excess of the natural consequences of your actions, and vice versa for bad things, when you do not do what you want. It might even seem as if there's some kind of supernatural karmic force at play. Why? Perhaps the natural consequences of your actions are greater than you predicted; perhaps your perception of yourself influences how you perceive things to be happening to you, and/or which things you pay attention to; perhaps you subconsciously or consciously reward or punish yourself for your own actions; perhaps other people subconsciously or consciously perceive your attitude and treat you differently. Plausibly it's a little bit of all of these in concert. If you're willing to pay attention and see things as they really are, you will find that the appeal of doing what you want is incomparable, a disproportionate benefit compared to a disproportionate loss.

MOMENT OF CLARITY

Imagine a person with a half-decent conscience who has slipped into a low point in life, who is not doing what they want and is instead just floating from distraction to distraction, bad habit to bad habit, scarcely recognizable as a conscious living thing. That half-decent conscience will eventually start churning out guilt and shame, a perfectly natural response to such circumstances; and if the timing is right, a true moment of clarity may occur, a moment when a person finally says "that's enough, it's time to make a change."

It's very possible in such moments to suddenly figure everything out, to understand that the real barrier to progress has been oneself the entire time. After some moment of intense, stressful thought, after some collapse of one's ability to distract oneself, and after a thorough contemplation of one's real issues, solving them may abruptly seem incredibly easy. It may be revealed that solving them was easy all along, and that the only thing missing was the essential first step of beginning to work on them. Perhaps they are mundane things like brushing one's teeth or washing the dishes, or perhaps more specialized things such as writing a college essay or making an important phone call for some business or other; nonetheless, once the first step has been taken, dealing with the thing in question is easy. Anyone who has ever procrastinated on an essay for weeks only to finish it in two hours knows this feeling well. One might just as easily find that any ordinary task of life, which one might have put off and quietly agonized over in a distracted state for days and weeks and months on end, may be easily over and done with in only an hour, if not less.

And when everything has been done, when one's to-do list has been reduced to nothing, when all of a sudden, weeks of accumulated stress have been eliminated at their source in an instant, the world suddenly seems remarkably comfortable and easy to live in. To people who have lived for many years in a squalid or depraved state and who are only just now consciously improving themselves, literally for the first time in their lives, this effect is magnified: compared to the rotten life of the past, where everything seemed so difficult and nothing seemed to ever get done, a magnificent sense of potential appears, the slate has been wiped clean, past sins against oneself forgiven, as if all the troubles of the world have disappeared, and one is finally at peace to simply sit and relax, satisfied.

At least for a moment. At least while one has actually ceased these bad habits, and at least while one has actually taken care of these important items of what would otherwise be unfinished business. If the calm and peaceful sensation produced by this achievement is simply used as a backdrop for unthinking relaxation, and one does not continue to designate regular attention to the ordinary maintenance of one's life, how easy it is to completely sink back into the exact same state of procrastination and inadequacy as before! How easy it is to bask in the clean and pleasant sensation produced by having accomplished some actual work, to say to oneself "I deserve a reward," and to promptly cease to do everything which produced that blissful sensation in the first place! In a few weeks, one might have found that the condition of one's life has gone around in a complete circle, with no overall progress having been made whatsoever. How many New Year's resolutions fail according to this exact pattern?

A cycle of this sort may be repeated who knows how many times before a person decides to actually make a lasting change. Dozens of times? Hundreds? It's not impossible that a person might let it go on forever, never changing at all in the long term. To get anywhere in life, to make any change toward the direction of living how you want to live, doing what you want, bad habits must be broken and good habits must be constructed and practiced. This is all common knowledge, but as usual for common knowledge, it's rarely practiced. Some changes can be made all at once, others are more difficult and must be carefully implemented over time, not being too hasty or too hesitant. Bad habits in particular are difficult to break once ingrained; drug addiction and food addiction even more so. But even these latter cases can be overcome, even if they do require you to seek and accept outside help (from friends, a doctor, or what have you). It is only a matter of recognizing that you want to do it, and of taking what you want seriously.

FAILURE TO BE SELF-CRITICAL

There are some who would say that to be unrelenting with self-criticism is cruel, that it is liable to make you hate yourself. But if you cannot honestly evaluate your life without hating yourself, then you must hate yourself. To do otherwise would be a lie. But don't just continue hating yourself like an idiot, or worse, hate yourself for a minute and then return to your old equilibrium. The only solution that will satisfy you in the end is this: make yourself so perfect that you no longer need to hate yourself. Let your hatred of your failures be aligned with your desire for success. Do what you want, don't do what you don't want. This is not a great revelation. This is not groundbreaking. This is obvious. If it seems novel to you, maybe you should make a habit of thinking about things that you want, as opposed to... well, whatever else it is that you spend your time thinking about.

If you cannot stand the "cruelty" of acknowledging and criticizing your real situation, then you will be crushed under the weight of your inadequacies. However much you might try to distract your conscious mind from your failures, from the existence of your poor choices, and from your failure to acknowledge the resulting issues, the fact of their existence will remain in your unconscious mind whether you like it or not. Your unconscious mind is a terrifying thing to have as an adversary – and it is your adversary, if you try to live in denial of the things that it has come to understand, of the troubles that it has seen, but which you, the conscious one, have left unaddressed. It is a frightening and intriguing fact that the human brain can experience emotions *without the individual consciously understanding why.* This is one potential source of anxiety disorders; the individual feels all of the symptoms of extreme fear, of catatonic panic, but without knowing what it is that their "body" (really the unconscious mind) seems to be afraid of. This could be a completely idiopathic response, the brain and body experiencing a strange emotional response for absolutely no discernable reason. But perhaps it's more common that, in such a situation, the unconscious mind has picked up on some kind of anxiety-inducing stimulus that the (conscious) individual has not yet acknowledged, either due to lack of attention or overt denial. This is only one example of the unconscious mind's remarkable power. To live in denial, perhaps by ignoring your problems or perhaps by artificially lowering your standards for yourself (that is, below a level that you are actually comfortable with experiencing), is to invite this type of problem and a host of others.

Try though you might to dissolve your consciousness in distractions, of either the social or asocial variety, there will always be a "you" which feels unsatisfied, if what you're doing is not what you truly want. As long as your brain is not hopelessly impaired, you will retain your conscience, you will hear in the back of your mind that little voice that says, when you are tempted by certain things,

"This is a bad idea." How often is this voice, this daemon of Socrates, incorrect in its warning? In my personal experience, I can't think of a single occasion. And as this little warning occurs for individual incidents, a more massive sensation of dread looms after weeks and months and years wasted, spent carelessly on such bad ideas. Neither the little voice nor the great thunderstorm will disappear unless you destroy your brain entirely. Rather than do this, is it so unreasonable to simply be realistic and honest? Yes, of course it is reasonable, but for so many people, it's just so *easy* to be unreasonable, to not care about reason and reality and honesty, to ignore the future and "live in the moment" in the worst possible sense of the phrase.

LABELS OF GOOD AND EVIL

Be careful not to jump too quickly to the words "good" and "evil." Be careful not to label things with these labels too rapidly. There may be a way that you have always used these words, a way that you simply considered "the truth" of right and wrong, something that you've been told (and that you've told yourself) since childhood; these things are also on the chopping block. Even these deep notions of good and evil are subsidiary to what you want.

It's very easy to habitually insist that something simply *is* a certain way; but in order to be honest, you must think critically. Don't stamp a unilateral label on something just because it has certain elements about it that you have been taught to call "good" or "evil." It doesn't matter whether the source of this labeling schema is tradition, convention, or aesthetics: no such thing should take priority over using your brain to determine the nature of things, and to determine their relation to what you want.

When you are tempted to jump to a quick judgment, an immediate framing of something as "evil," stop yourself and think about it. Perhaps this is a hasty decision. In the end, is this thing, which some might call "evil," actually harmful? Is there actual malice or hatred in it? Is there any harm that will come of it? Who will be harmed by it? Can you concretely describe the process of harm, from start to finish, without speculating or exaggerating? There are certain ideas which, once stuck in a person's head, are difficult to get out – even if they became stuck in there for an unsound reason. Could it be that a portion of your ideas about right and wrong are like this? Not what you truly believe, but merely something stuck in your head?

There are certain people who consider themselves morally righteous because they are so valiantly opposed to "evil;" under their worldview, they label a very large number of things as "evil," and so they have many opportunities to loudly proclaim how much they hate all these evil people and how terrible they all are. It's easy to understand that people can and do act like this under false pretenses. It's harder to understand that you may be doing this yourself, inadvertently, ultimately stemming from a simple cause such as your aesthetic tastes (recall the section "Projection and Propaganda" from Part III). If you find yourself spending a lot of time railing against evildoers, and a lot of your mental energy thinking about them, be sure to put your beliefs to the test, weighing the possibility of giving them up – even if you've already invested a lot of time and money into them. It's never too late to run a test to see whether your response is really warranted – dropping your opinion and starting from scratch may seem unpleasant, but sprinting full-tilt into an opinion you don't really believe in is a far more dangerous risk. In general, you don't want to fill your life with more negative emotion and animosity than necessary. Life is already difficult enough; why go out of your way to make yourself even more unhappy? That being said, if you should find something to be very aesthetically unappealing but not technically malicious, there's no obligation for you to involve yourself with it or promote it; that is a matter of taste. But you should probably be willing to tolerate its existence, if only for practical reasons; namely, in order to avoid wasting your valuable time and mental energy seething over something that's merely ugly, and not an actual problem.

And just as being quick to use the word "evil" leads to excessive forbidding, being quick to use the word "good" (in the superlative sense) leads to excessive mandating. Forbid too harshly, and you may end up forbidding yourself from something you want; mandate too earnestly, and you may end up mandating for yourself something you don't want. You don't want to wind up as the person who neurotically denies their true desire, saying to themselves that they are not orthodox enough, that they are not radical enough, or that they are not neutral enough – bemoaning that they are not "good" enough, and that within them is "evil."

Even your basic ideas about good and evil, which you may consider too fundamental to be questioned, deserve all the more to be questioned. If these things are truly your beliefs, beliefs in accordance with what you want, then so be it; but if they are not, if you have simply fooled yourself, or been fooled by someone else, into believing in them, then yes, even these things must be cast away – and replaced with tougher, hardier ideas. How, then, to tell the difference? This book has said so again and again: be skeptical, be realistic, and be honest. Think "with a hammer," as Nietzsche said; let those ideas fall away which are not strong enough to stand up to a thorough pummeling. If your childhood memories have not been too deeply buried, you should be able to recall times in your youth when you believed something without a good reason; and when it became apparent that it was not worth believing, what happened? Either the belief was dropped all at once, or slowly shaved away, piece by piece. Did you once believe in Santa Claus, for example? Or that some adult was a perfect person? Or did you have some completely nonsensical belief about the facts of the natural world? Remember that such beliefs were yours yesterday; do not cling too tightly to any particular belief simply because it is yours today. A belief may simply be a childish thing that you picked up one day and never learned to throw away. Question even those ideas that you would be tempted to call unquestionable. The best ideas will be able to stand up to this questioning. As for those that are not able to – "commit them to the flames."

ANIMAL

Those who wish to be virtuous people must handle their ideals carefully. It is very possible for someone to live with their head in the clouds, always thinking of their "higher self," fantasizing about what life might be like as a perfect being, something free from the limitations of the human animal. Or they may imagine what "perfect behavior" would be like, what they could do if they could only get rid of these annoying animalistic temptations. But these ways of thinking are self-defeating, because human beings are animals.

The existence of the human species would not have been possible without our ancestors having certain self-sustaining psychological inclinations. An animal must eat in order to survive, and must mate in order to reproduce. An animal must gather and protect resources in order to ensure its own survival, and an animal must recognize when others are better off, and must wish itself to be better off than others, in order to survive in a competitive environment. An animal must refrain from expending excessive energy in order to survive when food and/or body fat are scarce, or when predators seek to catch exhausted prey unawares. An animal must fight when cornered, to defend its own life. And most importantly, to survive in any capacity, to take any action conducive to its own survival, an animal must prioritize itself, it must consider itself fundamentally important. The feelings and urges associated with all of these things are necessary for the survival of any animal remotely similar to a human being. Without these things, you would not be alive; these things are not bad or evil *per se*, they are not things to try to minimize, they are not things to try to avoid at all costs. Because you are an animal, these things are a part of you. Not something foreign or abnormal which happens to be attached to you, like a disease, but a *part of you* as much as any other part of your mind. In fact, you could even make the case that these traits are *more so* a part of you than the parts that you would be happy to advertise on a resumé: if you had been raised in a different time or place, by different people or otherwise under different conditions, many of your personality traits and intellectual qualities would turn out different, but your instinctive desires would be the same. They are more quintessential to your person, in that sense.

You are an animal, and there is no getting around it. The psychological phenomena which allowed your ancestors to survive, these instincts and urges, are present within you, a part of what you are. To consider such things to be unacceptable, or worse yet, "unnatural," is denying your own nature, it is denying the fact that you are an animal. Denying this is denying reality, and this will not get you very far in reality. Fantasizing about being some kind of angel, a creature immune to vulgar temptation, is no different than fantasizing about gaining the power of telekinesis: it simply will never happen, and there is no working towards making this fantasy a reality. You can try to repress your animal instincts, but you can never stop being an animal. Maybe, millions of years from now, the descendants of humanity will be some kind of *2001: A Space Odyssey*-esque higher life form, and they will not have those characteristics that would offend Puritans; but this is a long way off. As of today, every person on Earth is an animal.

It's important to be realistic about this. Those who would style themselves as totally virtuous, morally perfect, fully rational, or some other such fantasy, will find themselves wracking their brains to try to explain their own animal nature – "Why, if I am so good, do I want to do such bad things?" Every human being has secrets, every human being has pleasures which do not fit in with the "normal way of living" that is the consensus of their local civilization, and which the people around them treat as the *de facto* ideal of virtue. It's one thing to resist temptation and refrain from performing certain actions at certain times – but to deny that temptations are part of oneself in the first place? That is denial of one's own nature, and that is begging for trouble.

A person who lives in denial about their nature could develop all sorts of weird psychological problems, tying their mind in knots, trying to cling to positions that lead to cognitive dissonance while reality, unmoving, seems to assault them at every turn. Someone unwilling to tolerate their own animal nature might, for example, live a cyclical life, alternating between periods of repression and indulgence of the various temptations that crop up within them. The person behaves in a very nice, orderly fashion for a while as they tell themselves that they are done, that the animal will no longer tempt them, that they are finally a good person, a person of fine moral character. This repression, however, quickly gives way to indulgence, a wanton casting-off of their shackles of morality, pleasures ravenously chased in some secret place. The person shifts irresistibly from the former to the latter as if pushed by the invisible hand of fate, but in fact they are pushed by desires that are *their own,* and the moral part of their mind simply pretends not to notice this. Only after the desire has been sated is the person's reasonable, decent character, which pompously calls itself their "true self," allowed to return to the forefront of the mind. "Reason is, and ought to be, the slave of the passions," says Hume. Joyce's *Portrait of the Artist* describes this phenomenon in a young man, who, for reasons he refuses to acknowledge, periodically indulges in that for which he says "he was not worthy to be called God's child," that which he calls more shameful than murder, a most grave and unnatural sin: having sex with women. Hesse's *Steppenwolf* outlines something similar in an erudite middle-aged man. Though it is not quite as explicit with what constitutes his "wolfish" activities, it is said that the protagonist lived two lives, one as a man, and one as a Steppenwolf, a wolf of the steppes, and that his life (as of the beginning of the novel) consisted of the two souls alternately controlling his body.

There is no sense in denying that which is unavoidably a part of you. Though it may be in bad taste to brag about feeding what are called your base instincts, you must nonetheless feed them. Don't overfeed them, of course – but feed them. They are part of you, and feeding them is part of feeding yourself. The idea is moderation, not abstinence. Sure, there will be certain particular things that you will want to abstain from, but no part of you should be starved to the point of mortification. To pretend to be an angel is to deny being human. Now, some would use this fact as an excuse to do the opposite, to give into their every dark desire, and to live a life of fake hedonism, or worse, outright sadism; but this is also not satisfactory, for obvious reasons. Those who are not plagued by guilt over their depravity will be plagued by the consequences of their actions, perhaps including encounters with the police, or some other vengeful adversary. Balance is the word.

If you have a flair for dramatic language, *a la* Blake or Nietzsche, you could describe these simple, animalistic parts of you with a phrase like "your evil" or "your shadow," in contrast to the intellectual, moral, sophisticated parts of you which you might call "your good" or "your light," the combination of which make up "all of you." And the idealistic fantasizing which denies being human, mentioned just before, you could describe that as "rejecting the gift of life." Refer to these things how you like, just remember not to confuse poetic license with reality. If "evil" means real maliciousness, characterizing instinctive or self-serving traits generally as "evil" is misleading. If you haven't eaten for 24 hours, is it evil for you to want to eat a lot of food? If someone punches you, is it evil to want to punch them back? No.

INTEGRATION

Living a one-sided life will not work, no matter how clean and presentable you make that one side. It is balance, moderation, integration of your whole personality into the works of your life, which is the way to what you want. There will be times at which it almost seems as if you do not have that animalistic, instinct-driven, tempting personality at all – but at those times, you must not be tempted by the words of your polite, calm, moral personality that tells you that it, and only it, is *your true self*, and that the other thing is *not you*. You are all of you. Everything that you do is done by you. Denying this leads to the *Dr. Jekyll and Mr. Hyde* situation, where you pretend that a part of you isn't you, and you consequently don't consider yourself responsible for what it does – but this leaves it (or, more accurately, you) totally unleashed and more liable than ever to cause trouble. For your own sanity's sake, accept the truth and let the different parts of you work together, so all of you can be happy.

There are exceptions to this rule, but they are rare. A small number of people are out there who can tolerate a monastic lifestyle, a life totally separated from what you might call "earthly temptations," because, due to some quirk of personality, they simply do not feel tempted by them. They can live this different way of life, with its advantages and disadvantages; meanwhile, lots of other people will idealize this kind of life and role-play as this unusual character, while actually harboring the usual suite of personality traits, temptations and all. If such a role-player dedicates themselves to such a life, they could go quite a distance along this path, fueled by stubbornness alone – but they won't find their achievements satisfying, because this lifestyle necessitates the denial of something that they, deep down, *truly do want*, loathe though they may be to admit it in polite conversation. If someone convinces themselves that such-and-such thing is the "best" or "highest" goal in life, and they spend years pursuing it, only to receive no real satisfaction – how can they believe any other thing in life will be satisfying? The Question rears its ugly head once again. You can lead a life with clean and wholesome goals, but if you're not one of those exceptional people, it's probably a bad idea to try to do so to the exclusion of everything else. To be completely fair, though, you can (and maybe even *should*) test yourself to see if you are such a person, to see if you can actually tolerate such a thing or not – just make sure the decisions you make are reversible in case it doesn't work out; don't put all your eggs in one basket.

Concerning this idea of integration, a reader may object: "What if I want to become a serial killer? How am I supposed to integrate something like that into my life?" Much like the objection in a previous section, the question to ask in response to this is: do you actually want to become a serial killer? Is that actually what you want, to destroy a bunch of people's lives and eventually, in all probability, get caught and thrown into a maximum-security prison? And the same goes for any other desire for an extreme act of cruelty: if you truly think about it, is this actually what you want to do with your life?

The question above is not rhetorical; it is actually a serious question that deserves serious consideration, if the objecting reader is serious and not just being pedantic. A question like this can't be solved by appeals to morality, because it's not as if, to the person seriously wrestling with such a desire, "having morals" in the conventional sense would cause their deepest immoral desires to go away. Instead, let us focus on pure practicality, at least for starters. Is this way of life actually going to be satisfying? Is it what you want, is it what you believe would be best for you? Any readers who aren't completely mad with bloodlust will answer no; as for those who are, well, there's not much I can do as a writer to try to convince them of anything. They already know the risks, and they might even find pleasure in considering themselves villains. Whatever I could tell them in terms of morality, they've already heard it a thousand times before. This book is for those who are not completely beyond salvation. I'll add three notes, though, just in case: First, don't be quick to assume that you, yourself, are completely beyond salvation. This would be making excuses, not being genuine, submitting to a simple desire rather than exerting your real power, letting your weakness cause destruction, like a child throwing a tantrum. Second, it is possible that the root of the desire to perform extreme acts of destruction could be something not specifically destructive, but rather something more elementary, like "the desire to exert power over others;" this could conceivably be sublimated into something more productive, something both beneficial and gratifying to the one who loves exerting power. Third, if you often indulge in fantasies of extreme and violent acts, maybe it is only *fantasizing itself* which is gratifying to you – perhaps doing the real thing would be too much, would drive you beyond regret and into insanity, as was the case for Dostoyevsky's Raskolnikov, and Nietzsche's "pale criminal" from the first part of *Zarathustra.*

To more directly address the principle in question, the suggestion that a serial-killer level of malice can't be meaningfully integrated with a generally benevolent life is pretty obviously correct. There are some people who commit both remarkable acts of cruelty and remarkable acts of charity in a single lifetime – a billionaire can engage in humanitarian philanthropy and knowingly capitalize on slave labor simultaneously; a director, musician, or other artist can produce magnificent works in their medium of choice, all the while moonlighting as a vicious sex criminal; and those who are not especially rich or famous can do the same type of thing at a smaller scale. This weird duality is an attempt at a compromise between two parts of the self – not an alliance. The constant parade of scandals in politics and celebrity drama shows that acts of real malice cannot be hidden for long, even with all the protective measures that the rich can afford; once exposed, the culprit will be held responsible, and opportunities for future acts of good will be denied them. Such people sometimes have very public nervous breakdowns; compromises of this kind are hard for the conscience to stomach.

With that said, at the end of the day, what exactly is there to be done if you happen to have "evil" desires which are too powerful to ignore or repress? Let's investigate the second note from earlier in greater detail. It's possible for a person to use the motivations behind their "evil" inclinations to create some kind of important positive change in the world, such as an invention. Imagine that a person becomes a prodigious and dedicated software engineer and creates a revolutionary virtual reality technology, something which ends up being broadly adopted by various industries, and that goes on to help make millions of people's lives better – but the inventor's motivation, their secret, personal motivation, was to make their dream video game, an ultra-realistic VR serial rapist simulator. It wouldn't be the first time something good was invented for a bad reason. Strange though it might seem, even the most destructive inclinations have the potential to be transmuted into something beneficial.

If all of this can be said in the defense of the person who is literally contemplating something as extreme as serial killing, how much easier will it be to defend your own instinctive, self-serving desires? If this much hope exists for even that kind of person, how much more confidence can you have that you can find a way to successfully make your so-called "dark side" into something you can work with productively, creatively, and pleasurably? Let this fact encourage you to refrain from that moral compromise, that false separation, that framing of your animal instinct as something foreign, something that is "not you." What it wants is a part of what you want, because it is a part of you. The object is to do what you want; examine your options honestly and thoroughly, and see what it is that will best lead you to what you want. Avoid hastily using labels such as "good" or "evil" to mark potential paths forward as either mandatory or forbidden. Apply this principle to not just acquire, achieve, and become the portion of what you want that fits the aesthetic of "the good," but to acquire, achieve, and become *all of what you want.*

SACRIFICE

Often, when speaking about achieving great things, people will throw around the word "sacrifice." But this word, and the conceptualization that comes with it, is something that can make the execution of what you want more difficult. Every action comes with opportunity costs, and doing what you want is no exception. To do what you want, you must refrain from doing what you don't want. Is this what you call a "sacrifice"? It shouldn't be. To clean filth off of something is not "sacrificing" the filth in exchange for cleanliness. A drug addict in a rehabilitation program is not "sacrificing" their addiction in exchange for health. Removing your hand from a fire is not "sacrificing" the pain in exchange for pain's absence. The things that are obstacles to what you want should not be conceptualized as "sacrifices." If they have so little value that they must be discarded in order to achieve what you want, to speak of "sacrificing" them is to speak too fondly of them.

The word "sacrifice" calls to mind the image of ancient religious rituals, wherein the best of the livestock is slaughtered and burned in order to appeal to some god or gods. But, in order to do what you want, it is not the best that must be destroyed – but the worst. That which is a hindrance to what you want, that which gets in the way of what you want, must be cast out of the way.

Consider, for example, the attitudes that many people have towards diet and exercise, those fundamental components of maintaining physical and mental health. Some people are so averse to their own healthiness that they will consider any attempt at maintaining some kind of diet or exercise routine to be, rather than a means of voluntarily improving their lives, a mandatory sacrifice of their own happiness. Granted, this might occur because the person has the wrong idea entirely about how diet and exercise should be executed – but then again, it might occur because they actually are just plain lazy and unwilling to change, unwilling to think about the future and act toward their own long-term interests. A person who, in some circumstance, thinks that they "have to" sacrifice their own happiness should reevaluate what it really is that makes them happy, and what will bring them happiness in the long term. If being fat and lazy brings happiness in the short term, but misery in the long term, then perhaps living a sedentary lifestyle on a poor diet can be discarded – "sacrificed" is not the proper word. It is not a sacrifice to be rid of the things that cause you more pain in the long term. Inversely, suppose that you have some hobby or interest that provides you more pleasure than pain, but it's something often looked down upon, for example, something considered a juvenile or superficial form of entertainment. If a person swallows the idea that they have to get rid of everything "imperfect" in their lives, they might sacrifice this thing too, because they think they "have to" – even if it is not a problem in any tangible sense, and not actually an obstacle to what they want. Rest and relaxation are a part of life, and trying to rid yourself of the things that allow you to relax (either physically or mentally) will drive you insane. What you want is best achieved without sacrificing anything.

Now, what about the case where a person drops absolutely everything in life in order to become world-class at something, in some sport or art or business venture? This person is something of an exception to the rule, because it definitely does seem as if they sacrifice everything for one goal. But that's just it – this is the exception, not the rule, and the things they discard are indeed sacrificed. To sacrifice absolutely everything is to take a huge gamble, not only on one's natural proclivity towards learning the skills necessary to reach the pinnacle of this sort of achievement *and* to be able to keep up with the sheer quantity of work required *and* to be able to deal with the harshest competition, but also on the hope that nothing will go wrong. A person dedicates their entire life to a sport, gets into a car accident, their leg is broken, and when it heals it'll be far weaker than before, such that they can never play this sport on a professional level again. Now what? A person becomes the best in the world at manufacturing a certain specialized kind of product, and then a technological change happens and the entire industry is rendered unsustainable. Now what? It's a monumentally risky gamble to focus absolutely on one thing, to have that thing be the subject of your entire life. But then again, there do exist world-class gamblers.

SILVER PLATTER

For almost anyone, constructing a stable baseline for your life is an important part of doing what you want. It's beneficial to have your life be at least somewhat organized, so that you can do the things you want without basic problems getting in your way. This is useful, legitimate advice for almost everybody. There do exist rare artists who can only produce their art while suffering, while in destitute or chaotic circumstances, and who would actually be hindered from creating their art by trying to add stability. But these are exceptional cases. In the typical case, it is useful to have a good degree of order in one's life, and plenty of people will be happy to give you this advice – but this advice is not the end. This advice only represents the first few steps towards obtaining what you want, and it is possible to cling to these first steps and refuse to go any further. A person can construct a very stable, balanced lifestyle, free from debt, away from abusive people, keeping all basic life responsibilities covered, and even being what you might call "successful," but without actually doing what they want.

There will come a time, once you have created a stable baseline for your life, and when you have worked on yourself for a while, when what you want is finally within your reach. You have overcome every barrier and crossed every threshold, and what you want is now directly in front of you, being served to you on a silver platter, and the only thing left is to reach out and take it. But many people, even in this position, will fail to do so. Perhaps you are tired from your long journey and want to rest on a nearby sofa, even fall asleep for a while; and perhaps you will say that this is "to ensure that you have the energy" to, at another time, raise your arm, reach out, and take what is directly in front of you. How long exactly do you intend to sleep? If you take your eyes off of the silver platter for too long, the server carrying it will note your disinterest and take it to another room, perhaps to another guest who wishes to claim it for himself.

Alternately, perhaps you have grown so used to what you want *not* being in front of you that you cannot believe your eyes when it actually *is* in front of you. Perhaps you are so used to there being obstacles and prerequisites between you and what you want that you cannot believe your eyes when there are none left. So, you imagine that what is in front of you is not actually what you want, and that it's a fake, and so you scour the room for the real thing, even venturing into other rooms. Or perhaps you imagine that the room has been booby-trapped, ready to spring upon you as soon as you reach for the platter, and so you start searching for hidden devices. Or perhaps you imagine that the server holding the platter is secretly your strongest adversary, prepared to deliver a lethal blow if you should reach your hand out, and so you go into another room to physically train yourself in preparation for the fight. Or perhaps you imagine that what you want can only be taken at a very specific time, so you start inspecting the paintings and decoration around the room, looking for encoded clues on what that perfect time is. Or perhaps you believe that it is not proper to take what you want until the room you are in is immaculately clean, so you start dusting the shelves and washing the windows, often leaving the room to gather cleaning supplies, and taking additional time to groom and dress yourself up to the occasion. Again, while you are preoccupied with these imaginary obstacles, the server will notice your disinterest in taking what you want, and will move to another room. In any case, by the time you look again, the server has left, and you did not see where he went. It will now take even further exploration and surpassing of further obstacles just to reach the point where you were before.

It's good to sleep, but at some point, you will need to wake up. It's good to be prepared, but at some point, you will need to finish preparing and start acting. It's good to be organized, but at some point, you will need to do something with this organized space you've created. It is possible to focus too much on the basics. It is even possible to pretend that you're lacking information about how to do what you want, and to spend time thinking and thinking about what you already know – when you actually already know exactly how to do what you want, and the thing you are lacking is not information at all, but *action*. At some point, once the basics are known, understood, and implemented, the tools of dealing with the basics can be shelved, and you can dedicate your time to things beyond.

THE DEATH YOU WANT

Death is unavoidable. If you aim to conduct your life in the way you want, from start to finish, then the aim includes the finish – the end of what you want is the kind of death you want.

Philosophers of many different persuasions have stated this explicitly, including Plato (*Phaedo*), Montaigne ("That to Philosophize Is to Learn to Die") and Nietzsche ("Of Voluntary Death" from *Zarathustra*). It is a completely natural conclusion: if someone has achieved what they want in life, will they not accept death whenever it happens to arrive? If someone's mind is full of torment as they die, is that not a clear sign that there are things in life which they had desperately wanted to do, but had left undone?

Many readers will know the poem which runs:

"Do not go gentle into that good night,
Old age should burn and rave at close of day;
Rage, rage against the dying of the light."

Do these words appear to justify and sanctify a furious attitude in the old and dying, up until the last breath? The following stanzas certainly do not. Only those whose words have "forked no lightning," those who saw what deeds of theirs *might have* been, those who recognized their failures too late; only these, the poet writes, rage against the dying of the light. Rage is for the young, who can yet act well before the light dies; Rage is for those still able to absorb and reflect this light to the achievement of great ends. Once death's door is reached, there is no option but to be gentle – and any rage which has been saved until then is merely the twitching of a crushed insect. Whoever has done what they want, who has burned with passion while still capable of exercising their power, will not need to rage at close of day, but will indeed go gentle into that good night.

Planning for death is unlike planning for other parts of life. There is no planning for what to do during the moment of death, or for what to do afterwards; there is only planning for what to do beforehand, given the fact that it will happen, and that this will be the end, that the game will be over.

Under what circumstances do you wish to die? What will you reflect on, who will be near you, what method of death would be most appropriate? Or, if death should strike you suddenly, by some terrible accident, what will you reflect on in your final moments of consciousness? As death is an absolute, pondering these questions can help a person to understand what they want in the long term – begin at the end, begin at that which is absolutely certain, and work backwards. What is required to reach your desired ending? What ideas and potentialities today should be considered priorities, worked on immediately, while you are still young? Which ones, if left undone until your dying day, would leave you full of misery and regret? The consideration of death as something to plan for is not only useful in the general acceptance of death (that is, avoiding the pattern of living in denial, and learning to think beyond the short term), but also as a tool for isolating what you want in life. These will, in turn, help to inform your opinion on the Question itself – suicide.

AT THE EDGE

The last temptation is oblivion. At the edge, at the height of suffering, the most extreme of all options becomes visible to the person who previously hid from it, who refused to see it as an option. And now, it looms over the head of the open-minded one, as an option, as the most extreme possible exercise of one's freedom. But though one is free to perform the act, the act destroys all freedom. It is a "liberation" with no fruit, the finality of all restrictions and futility, cementing failure as failure, a state from which no great transformation or redemption can occur. It is the task of the person on the edge, who now admits that this most extreme option is an option, to not fall into tunnel vision at this critical juncture, to recognize how many other previously unconsidered options are now available, to be conscious of how unfathomably great the freedom of a human life truly is. If a person is not open-minded enough to understand that death is an option, they block themselves, by the same closed-mindedness, out of many other options in life – a person who actually *is* open-minded enough to face death directly should use their newfound vision to its greatest potential, and actually see the other options for what they are.

The inclination to cling to the status quo, to insist upon life and refuse death as an option, will hinder many people from becoming open-minded in this fashion until, perhaps, their intellect is overwhelmed by suffering – but once death is consciously acknowledged, once the fact of the Question is overcome, then the mind is liberated, the eyes more open than before. Every mentally mature person has wrestled with the Question. By acknowledging the Question, new truths are revealed; with new knowledge, growth is possible. It is possible to destroy a useless and ugly life without dying, to instead sublimate such a life, to transform it into something great. Once death itself is understood as an option, *everything else* can be understood as an option. If even one's most outrageous, diabolical, once-thought-impossible fantasies are on the table – perhaps death can wait.

I have said all I can on the subject of suicide. What comes after this in the confrontation of the Question cannot be spoken of from person to person, let alone told from writer to reader. All that remains after this will occur in the mind of the person facing the edge, the mind in its deepest solitude, at its most open and free, in meditations unbothered by any outside influence, in silent contemplation of everything, past, present, and future.

LAST WORDS

I imagine that this book will seem pessimistic to some readers, but it is only pessimistic concerning the welfare of those who cannot be bothered to think, those who choose not to think, and those who lie to themselves by pretending to be unable to think. A myriad of lies is available to the public; they are easily acquired and easily swallowed, and with terrible ease another mind is made narrower, another mind is convinced that it has no choice, that it has to do this, that it must never do that. But these lies sit harshly in the stomach, and must be vomited out at some point if the pain they induce is ever to end. One must be careful to consider nothing as absolutely, unquestionably true, and to understand the true meaning and extent of open-mindedness and honesty.

There is nothing more frightening than futility, and there is nothing more wretched than the person who imposes an imaginary futility upon themselves. The one who is too afraid to confront the question of suicide does not understand their own freedom, and so they are too afraid to exercise their freedom, too afraid to live. They may remain alive in the technical sense, but properly speaking, they are dying more than living: committing suicide by indifference.

To try to convince a person to live rather than simply remain alive, all kinds of media are saturated in carrots – but these mean nothing without the stick. The stick is the profound ugliness and needless misery of the person who considers themselves a slave to life, a person consigned to never live, but to voluntarily submit to avoidable hardships in exchange for the privilege of remaining alive, and/or some spurious promise concerning the next life. This is the nobody who considers themselves fundamentally separate from every somebody of the past and present. But every somebody began as a nobody – yes, even those born into great wealth and privilege. No matter how much money you have, you have to live, you have to do what you want, in order to become a somebody. A rich person can do absolutely nothing for their whole life; and many do, becoming entirely forgotten after one generation. If you live in a rich nation, you too are probably considerably richer than the average resident of this planet. If it's wrong for a celebrity to waste their privileges on a vapid life, will you put your own privileges to better use?

To survive without living, to refuse that which you consider best and which you want the most, is a life of failure, if it can be called a life at all. "For what should it profit a man that he should gain the whole world, and lose his soul?" Or, if you still sacrifice your true self but are too "good" to at least get some kind of mundane wealth or status or pleasure for it, then: "Your worst sin is that you destroyed and betrayed yourself for nothing." Keep your soul, and do not destroy or betray yourself; those who would sacrifice themselves, whether for a misguided ideal or for fear of offending others, will find themselves crushed, destroyed, dead - only alive in the sense of having a heartbeat.

To do what you want is to live. The maxim "be yourself" does not mean "be what you already are," but "be what you want to be." If you want something done at all, do it yourself. If you do not do what you want, nothing that you want will ever happen. If you do not think about the future, you will suffer when the future arrives. All of this is obvious. Every experience you have, if you can be bothered to think, will affirm this. To deny the facts is to lie to yourself, to pull yourself down, to cling to the scraps of the short-lived bliss that occasionally interrupts the overwhelming suffering of ignorance. To say to yourself that you accept the facts, but to do nothing about them, is perhaps even stupider. To accept the facts of life, to live beyond mere survival, and to bring an Answer into reality is nothing long or short of this: to do what you want. Those who spend their lives in the pursuit and achievement of what they want will reach, at the time of death, the enviable condition of being able to truthfully pronounce these last words: "No regrets."

www.ingramcontent.com/pod-product-compliance
Lightning Source LLC
LaVergne TN
LVHW010654110826
845149LV00014B/3089

* 9 7 9 8 9 9 9 9 4 6 7 0 6 *